POWER TO BECOME

What God Wants You To Be

POWER TO BECOME
What God Wants You To Be

GYNNATH FORD

Christian Communications
P. O. Box 150
Nashville, TN 37202

Published by Christian Communications
A division of the Gospel Advocate Co.
P. O. Box 150
Nashville, TN 37202

ISBN 0-89225-306-1

INTRODUCTION

In 1966 a minister in England stepped into the pulpit with a wash basin, a towel, soap, and a razor. He shaved himself without saying a word and then sat down. A murmur spread throughout the congregation. After the service he was questioned about this strange behavior. He replied, "I wanted to do something so fantastic, so out of the ordinary, so unexpected that every person would go out and talk about it. I wanted everyone's friends to hear about it. I wanted it to spread throughout the country. I wanted every person to catch the flavor of what it was like the Sunday the news spread about the risen Christ!"

My aim in writing this book is to enable you to catch the flavor of what power you possess as a child of God. I want you to do something 95 percent of people do not do—set goals and know where you are going. I want you to feel good about yourself, regardless of whether you feel you are failing or succeeding at the present time. I want you to learn how to dream dreams and then to realize them. I want you to experience the blessings that can come from giving yourself away.

My thanks go to the following people: Jack Exum, who motivated me to write this book and deliver this material all over this land; Robert Overton, my father-in-law, who introduced me to Ron Willingham's

Success for You course; Jim and Ruby Williams, who shared a business with me which has brought mountains of motivation to my mind and has brought me into contact with some very successful people; and my lovely wife, Ruth, who has believed in me for over three decades and has challenged the best in me to come alive. Thank you, God, for all of these and others who have made me what I am today.

Gynnath Ford

CONTENTS

CHAPTER 1

POWER TO DREAM

God wants men to dream. The Bible says, "... Your old men shall dream dreams ...." (Acts 2:17). Baylor University Coach Brian Teaff was directing a marriage encounter seminar. He challenged the group to write a goal for ten years in the future. His question was, "How do you see yourself ten years from now?" An elderly gentleman who had been married for sixty-five years smiled and wrote down his statement. He approached Mr. Teaff and asked, "Would you like to know what I wrote?" Coach Teaff smiled and nodded affirmatively. The older man replied, "I just hope I can see myself ten years from now!"

You may argue that it was not much of a goal. It was to him! Goals and dreams can keep you alive. Consider this: eight percent of people die within three months prior to their birthday, while forty-three percent die within three months after their birthday. Why? A mother says, "If I can just reach my ninetieth birthday, I'll be ready to go." Or, "If I can just live to see my family again at Christmas, I can die in peace." You say, that's not a very ambitious goal. Nevertheless, it is a goal and a dream which keeps people alive. What is your goal? What is your dream?

John enrolled in college and decided to become a preacher. He shared his dream with his roommate.

"I'm going to be a preacher." The roommate answered,
"John, you will never make it. You can't talk plainly,
and people will not listen to you." But John said, "I
don't care. I'm going to be a preacher." He had a dream.

There was a young lady on the campus whom John
admired. She was the homecoming queen and had
received several honors. John told his roommate, "I'm
going to date Mary Lou." His roommate laughed and
said, "John, she can go out with any guy on the
campus. She will not give you the time of day. Forget
it!" But John answered, "I don't care. I'm going to ask
her anyway." One day John approached Mary Lou and
said, "Mary Lou, I want to go out with you!" She
answered, "What did you say, John?" John repeated, "I
want to go out with you." She exclaimed, "John, you
are speaking distinctly! I can understand you per-
fectly! You must have been practicing to talk like this."
John replied, "I *thure* have. I've been practicing for
months!"

John had a date with Mary Lou! John became a
preacher! John married Mary Lou! Why? Because he
had dreams. John told someone about his dreams, and
then he did something about them.

Dream a dream. Tell a dream. Do a dream. Dreams
do come true! What God wants is a good person with a
dream.

I'm not telling you that if you have a dream and do
what you can to bring it about, that it will always come
true, especially if your dream involves another person. Mary Lou had a choice in the matter also. She
might have preferred Joe instead of John. But one
thing is true—only those who have dreams receive
their dreams. Go for it!

There is another reason you might not reach your
dream or goal. You have limitations. Everyone does, so
you are in good company. For instance, you might

never be an astronaut. Too old. Or you might never become a jockey. Too heavy.

Visualize yourself as an airplane. There are all types of airplanes—single-engine, two-engine, and super jets. All of these are designed to get off the ground and reach their potential. Although you do not know what model you are, God designed you to fly—figuratively speaking—to get off the ground and reach your potential. So begin dreaming about what you want to be and do. Dreams do come true! You can get off the ground!

In the past, God has provided dreams for some in a supernatural way. Joseph was one of these. God gave him a dream. The Bible says, "And Joseph dreamed a dream, and he told it to his brothers." Joseph dreamed a dream. Joseph told a dream. The Bible says, "And they hated him yet the more for his dreams and for his words" (Genesis 37). Be careful that you tell your dream to someone who will encourage you in it. Do not share it with a negative, critical person. He or she will *shoot it full of holes*. Tell it to someone who may have a similar goal or dream, and then support each other.

Later, the brothers of Joseph said, "Behold the dreamer comes." They sold him into slavery, but he became the best of slaves. He was framed by his master's wife and was thrown into prison, but he became the best of prisoners. He helped his fellow prisoner who was released. Joseph asked to be remembered, but he was forgotten. But in his providence, God brought Joseph out of that prison, and his dreams came true.

What kept Joseph going when his brothers treated him the way they did? What kept Joseph going when his master's wife treated him as she did? What kept Joseph going when he was serving time in prison?

He had a dream. He told this dream. He did

something about this dream. What did he do? He did what needed to be done, regardless of the circumstances. He did not become a negative, don't-care, sour-on-the-world, hateful person. He served wherever he was.

You might say, *"Wait a minute! That happened a long time ago."* That's right. *"God gave him a dream."* That's right. *"Well, I am not Joseph and I am not being prepared by God to lead His people."* How do you know you are not the one whom God can use? *"But that was different!"* Indeed it was. But Joseph was a real flesh-and-blood person who felt hurt when his brothers sold him. He felt hurt when his master's wife mistreated him. God could give him a dream, but Joseph had to believe that dream. That belief in God and his dream kept Joseph going.

Power of the Imagination

Do you still need convincing? What you want is proof that you can possess your dream in the twentieth century, right?

At one time, the whole earth was of one language and of one speech. Some people decided that the plan of God for their lives was not what they wanted. They said, "Let us build a city and a tower whose top may reach unto heaven, and let us make a name lest we be scattered abroad upon the face of the whole earth" (Genesis 11). And the Lord said, "Behold, the people are one, and they have all one language; and this they begin to do: and now nothing will be restrained from them which they have imagined to do." So the Lord confused their language. Notice what God said:

They are one (they are united).
They have one language (they are communicating).

They have imagination (nothing will be impossible).

What was one of the most powerful ingredients they possessed? Imagination. In this word are the words *image* and *in*. They had an image locked into their minds before they saw the tower begin to rise. You must have it in your mind and heart before you have it in your hand or life.

What did God say? Wicked people can plan and imagine and visualize and communicate and agree, and their dreams can come true. This is the reason evil conquers so many nations and people. There is great power in imagination.

God gave you one thing over which you can have complete control. You can't control your wife. You can't control your husband. You can't control your children as they get older. You can't control your neighbors. You can't control your brethren. But you can control your mind. It is *your* mind. You are what you are and where you are because of your thought habits. Your thought habits evolve from the food upon which your mind dwells. It is *your* mind. It was given to you by God as a servant to carry out your desires. No one may enter it and influence it in the slightest degree without your full consent and cooperation. Remember this fact when the circumstances over which you have no control move in and begin to bother you. Remember this when fear, doubt, and worry begin to park in the spare bedroom of your mind. God gave powerful minds to good people and to wicked people alike. This is the reason why Jesus talked so much about the heart. The Bible says, "For as he thinketh in his heart, so is he . . . ." (Proverbs 13:7).

Dreams can come true. If God permits wicked men to have dreams, and they have the power to carry them out, does He do less for His children, especially if it involves being a part of His plan for you?

Draw Pictures in Your Mind

A little girl was drawing a picture. Her mother asked, "Honey, what are you doing?" She replied confidently, "I'm drawing a picture of God." "Sweetheart, no one knows what God looks like." She, with a twinkle in her eye, replied, "They will when I get through." Whatever the child drew came from a figment of her imagination.

What we want to do is fertilize our imaginations. A leader in the Clearview church, Horace Litton, told of an experience he had when he was a boy. He said that only two people in the community had automobiles— the doctor and the mail carrier. He dreamed of an automobile. He said, "I felt that I would never be a doctor, but I could carry the mail." What do you think he is today? A rural mail carrier! That image was planted in his mind early in life. I have talked to numerous men who have told me that their mothers planted the seed of becoming a preacher in their minds. What did they become? Preachers!

> My mind is a garden,
> My thoughts are the seeds.
> My harvest will be
> Either flowers or weeds.
> —Mel Weldon

What do you see in your mind's eye?

Doug Hooper was teaching the power of visualization to inmates at Folsom Prison. To get a laugh, one of them said, "Why don't you try that stuff on Eugene?" Mr. Hooper said that they wanted him to make a public speaker out of the shyest individual there, one whom he had never heard speak at all. When Eugene came in, Mr. Hooper called him aside and encouraged him to participate in the experiment. He asked him to visualize himself as a great speaker giving a talk to these men and then receiving a standing ovation. Eugene sat quietly with his eyes closed for thirty minutes, then actually swaggered to the speaker's stand, pushed Mr. Hooper aside, gave a fine talk, and marched back to his seat. They gave him a standing ovation. He was never the same again. You must see it in your mind before you experience it in life.

Jesus did this when He first began preaching to his disciples. He said, "You are the light of the world." The disciples were anything but lights when He said that. But lights are what they became. You can too. Listen to Jesus. "Therefore I say unto you, what things soever you desire, when you pray, believe that you receive them, and you shall have them" (Mark 11:24). Jesus said that you have what you desire in your mind before you have them in your possession.

What do you want? What is the picture of the person you want to be? We know what we *don't* want. We don't want sickness, poverty, loneliness, rejection, and abuse. The real question is, what *do* you want? Decide what you want and plant that seed thought in your heart. See yourself accomplishing this particular work or becoming the person you have pictured in your mind.

What do you see? Do you see yourself as one who visits the sick, prays with and for them, leaving them with hope and good cheer? You say you have never been able to do *that* before in a satisfying way? You can and you will when you visualize yourself seated at their bedside with confidence and a smile. You might say, *"But I have never prayed with folks like that. What will I pray?"* Just say, "Father, bless my friend. In Jesus' name, Amen." We grew up on "God is great; God is good; God we thank you for our food." The Father loves short, simple, childlike prayers. You can do it!

Visualize yourself saying encouraging things to

your wife and children. Offer a "thank you" to your wife for the meal. When your children learn to ride the tricycles and say, "Whee, look at us," give them that compliment they need to succeed in life. Sometimes I ask children their grade in school. I have heard, "I'm in the eighth, but I ought to be in the ninth." Why do they say this? Because they are dwelling on their failures instead of their successes. You can help to change that by complimenting them on their successes.

Dr. Joe Harding tells a heart-warming story of a man who finally decided to ask his boss for a raise in salary. It was Friday. He told his wife that morning what he was about to do. All day the man felt nervous and apprehensive. Late in the afternoon he summoned the courage to approach his employer. To his delight, the boss agreed to a raise.

The man arrived home to a beautiful table set with their best china. Candles were lit. His wife had prepared a festive meal. Immediately he thought that someone from the office had tipped her off! Finding his wife in the kitchen, he told her the good news. They embraced and kissed, then sat down to a wonderful meal. Next to his plate the man found a beautifully lettered note. It read, "Congratulations, darling! I knew you'd get the raise! These things will tell you how much I love you."

While on his way to the kitchen to get dessert, he noticed that a second card had fallen from her pocket. Picking it up off the floor, he read: "Don't worry about not getting the raise. You deserve it anyway! These things will tell you how much I love you."

Visualize yourself as being a supportive mate, regardless of what life has to offer. See yourself accepting your loved ones in time of need, offering encouragement instead of discouragement. You say, *"That's not the way I am."* You can and will be that way when you paint this picture in your mind.

Think abut the power that will be unleashed when you draw a picture beforehand of the way you will react to criticism or conflict at work, home, or school. When you know that a critical issue is going to be discussed with your boss or loved one or critic, see yourself as being calm, cool, and collected, maintaining your poise and control at all times. Say aloud each day, "I can do all things through Christ who strengthens me" (Phillipians 4:13). You can do it!

Instead of harboring hatred in your heart for any enemy, see yourself praying for him and calling him by name before the heavenly Father. *"I can't do that,"* you say. You can and you will when you see yourself doing it.

Jesus forgave those who killed Him. I know a mother and grandmother who forgave the man who killed their young family member. That love and forgiveness contributed to his conversion, and he served his time in prison. He is now a faithful Christian serving society. Easy, no! Possible, yes!

What do you see? See yourself mowing a lawn for a widow. See yourself taking someone to the hospital to visit a loved one. Visualize yourself taking a friend to an Alcoholics Anonymous meeting. See yourself being successful in your business.

What do you see, teens? See yourself helping pick up books for someone in the hall at school. Visualize yourself befriending someone of another race or someone in a lower economic bracket, someone that others have shunned. See yourself being on time for every appointment and getting every assignment on time. You say, *"I can't do that."* You can and you will when you imagine yourself doing it!

What do you see? See yourself teaching the word of God to a friend. Visualize yourself praying for that friend every day. See yourself on the telephone cultivating a friendship. Imagine yourself inviting him to go to church with you. You can do it when you draw a picture in your mind of the event you want to come to pass.

Worthy Taylor hired a young lad named Jim to work on the farm. Jim lived in the barn. Mr. Taylor had a lovely daughter. Jim fell in love with her and asked for her hand in marriage. Mr. Taylor refused and said, "Jim, I admire you. You are a good worker. But I want my daughter to marry someone who is successful in life. I'm sorry."

Several years later, Mr. Taylor was tearing down the old, dilapidated barn. On one of the rafters Jim had carved his name, James A. Garfield, the name of the man who was at that time the President of the United States.

Mr. Taylor had never dreamed Jim was going to be that successful. Jim did not know it at the time he worked for Mr. Taylor. But the power was there. It was inside Jim, and it is inside you also. Somewhere along the way, Jim had a dream and did something about it. His dream came true. And your dream can too!

"Now unto him that is able to do exceeding abundantly above all that we ask or think, according to the power that worketh in us, unto him be glory in the church, by Christ Jesus, throughout all ages, worlds without end. Amen" (Ephesians 3:20,21).

The Bible says that there is a power in God's children that He can use and bring honor and glory to Him. Believe **this** and make your decision to dream a dream, tell a dream, and do a dream. Dreams do come true!

THINK ABOUT IT

1. What were the purposes of supernatural dreams in Bible history?
2. What are the counterparts of supernatural dreams in the church today?

3. Since you can't control other people, what is the best way to get them to do the Lord's will?
4. Write down two ways in which you have changed for good in the last ten years.
5. Select one day this week, begin in the morning, and make two lists of things you say that day. One list is positive and encouraging. The other list is negative and discouraging. Take personal inventory of the direction you are going—positive and negative.
6. List some characteristics of the men God chose to be communicators of His supernatural dreams or visions to man: Joseph, Daniel, John.
7. What is the most important step in getting started building your dream today?

CHAPTER 2

POWER TO BECOME

The power to become depends on me, but it does not depend completely on me. I like the positive support which the Philippian letter gives me. In the first chapter Paul says, "I am confident of this one thing, that God who has begun a good work in you will complete it. . ." (Phil. 1:6). This verse encourages me by stating that God is going to finish what He has started in me. In the second chapter Paul continues, ". . . God is the one who is working in you. How? He causes you to want to do what pleases him" (Phil. 2:13). This encourages me to realize that God motivates me. "And I have not already become perfect, but I press on to win what Christ Jesus won for me" (Phil. 3:12).

Sometimes I watch my favorite basketball team, Vanderbilt, play on late night TV. The game is in the final seconds and Vandy is four points behind. I am not tense. I am not stressful. Why? Because the game is a replay, and I know that Vandy has already won. Think what it means for us who are fighting in the battle of life against Satan. It looks like we are losing, but our spirits are lifted. Why? The victory has already been won by Jesus! The entire book of Revelation repeats this good news. Victory is ours! Stay in the fight! Don't give up! John writes, ". . . Greater is he that is in you, than he that is in the world" (I John 4:4). Satan may win some battles, but God has already won the war!

In the fourth chapter of Philippians, there is a verse which I repeat every day. It is a verse which I ask all who attend my seminars to repeat. It is a principle which revolutionizes the world of believers. "I can do all things through Christ who strengthens me" (Phil. 4:13).

Here is an acrostic of the words "I can."

> I —Imagination
> C —Commitment
> A —Affirmation
> N —Never Give Up

Let's examine each concept here.

I Can Use My Imagination

While speaking in Cuyahoga Falls, Ohio, I was given a copy of the remarkable story of a hostage named Jerry Levin who escaped from Lebanon. He was held in chains and blindfolded for nearly a year. He said that he willed himself to think only pleasant thoughts. He thought about his wife and children. He thought about his favorite pastime, grand opera, and how he could identify with some of the characters who had had to suffer as he was suffering. He thought about Beethoven, who had composed one of those operas. Beethoven had not let adversity—deafness—defeat him. He thought about the words of Beethoven, "I have never seen life as a resignation. Life is a gift, as the word is a gift from a generous God. As our vital strength is a gift, I will not submit. I shall have the courage of my endurance. Where my body fails, my spirit will dominate, my heart will create. I shall speak out of my silence. I shall shout! I shall sing! Man, help yourself! For you are able!"

Mr. Levin said that he saw nothing for nearly a year.

Yet, he did see! How? Through his imagination. And now he is a free man.

David Powell a minister friend of mine from West Virginia, tells this story. There was a greased pole contest at the fair. No one had won the fifty-dollar prize. David believed he could climb that pole. There were two reasons. He had done it before when he was younger. He had also visualized himself doing it. He won the prize. His brother-in-law, who was next in line to attempt it, said, "If you hadn't been first I would have done it." David replied, "You climb the pole, and I will give the fifty dollars to you." He couldn't do it. By the way, when you climb a greased pole, you slide down all the time. The secret is to climb twice as fast as you slide down, and not stop climbing even though you are sliding back down. Good lesson for life's setbacks. Keep climbing!

Olympic gold-medal pole vaulter Bob Richards said that every great champion, every great athlete he had ever met had a fixed goal or concept in his brain. When Bob was in the eighth grade, he was given a newspaper clipping of Dutch Warmerdam, the champion pole vaulter which he hung on the wall in his room. At the time he did this, he couldn't even beat the girls in running. But his imagination began to work for him.

My wife, Ruth, saw a house plan in a *Better Homes and Gardens* magazine. She kept that plan for fourteen years. She visualized living in that home. Her dream came true! Dreams do come true!

My mentor, Jack Exum, of Three Unusual Days fame, planted a seed in my mind when he wrote these words: "Take time and write that special book that's bottled up inside." I could see this book before it was ever written. I knew each chapter heading. I could see it being read by thousands like you!

Success for You author Ron Willingham, was writing the book *Life Is What You Make It* and got bogged down in the process. To stimulate his imagination, he had the jacket for the book made up beforehand and placed it over his typewriter. As he gazed upon it each day, he was motivated to complete the book.

In *God's Psychiatry,* Charles L. Allen tells of a teacher he discovered who teaches people to sit quietly and think of their minds as being absolutely blank. He tells them to think of the mind as a motion-picture screen. He says, "Flash on the screen of the mind a picture of something good you want to happen. Then take the picture off. Flash it on again. Take it off. Repeat that process until the picture becomes clear and sharp." Then he tells the student to go to work to make that picture a reality. It works!

Jesus fertilized the imagination of His disciples when He painted word pictures like this: "The kingdom of heaven is like a merchant man seeking goodly pearls, who when he had found one pearl of great price, went and sold all that he had and bought it. It is like a mustard seed which is the least of all seeds; but when it is grown, it is the greatest among herbs, and becomes a tree, so that the birds of the air come and lodge in the branches thereof" (Matthew 13).

When Jesus first began to preach, His disciples were still beginners. He challenged them with these words; "You are the light of the world. . . .

"You are the salt of the earth." And that is exactly what they became. But, first they had to see and imagine it in their hearts.

"I Can't Use My Imagination"

God believes in you, and He can't be wrong!

Do you ever worry? Do you anticipate something happening to you that is not good? Why, certainly you do! This is the power of using your negative imagination.

My daughter, Rebecca, is a freshman at David Lipscomb College. While attending a personal development course, she heard a classmate speak on the subject of worry. The young lady was very distraught as she told about two friends of hers who had been killed in separate auto accidents in the last six months. She was worried that she and her fiance would never get married because they might be killed in an auto accident. She was so overcome by the thought that she sobbed uncontrollably. One week later she missed class. She had been in an auto accident. She was back in school the next week with a neck support. What she thought about and feared had come to pass. This is the power of negative imagination.

You can use this same power to visualize good things rather than discouraging things. You can maximize your power of positive imagination.

I Can Be Committed

The second word in the acrostic is commitment.

In 1969, Fannie Lou Hamer received a special citation from Morehouse College in Atlanta, Georgia. Why? She had little formal education, and her speech was full of errors in grammar and diction. It was because she, a young black lady, had decided to go vote in a little town in Mississippi. When she arrived back at home after voting, her landlord and boss told her to withdraw her registration to vote or leave the farm. She left her husband there and moved to town. Ten days later sixteen bullets were fired into the home where she was staying. In Winona, Mississippi, Fannie Lou nearly lost her sight in one eye, and one of her kidneys was permanently damaged. She was also thrown in jail for helping others to register. Why did she persist? Because she was committed.

Jesus was committed before He came to planet Earth. The Bible says, "Let this mind be in you, which was also in Christ Jesus: who, being in the form of God, thought it not robbery to be equal with God: but made himself of no reputation, and took upon him the form of a servant, and was found in the likeness of men: and being found as a man, he humbled himself, and became obedient unto death, even the death of the cross" (Philippians 2:5-8).

Jesus made Himself nothing. He made Himself, the Bible says. He was not forced. He did not hold on to His exalted position. He became a slave to man here on earth. He was committed. He died the death of a common criminal. Even though He was the Son of God, He had no superhuman protection when He was a baby. He was in danger in Bethlehem, where the babies were killed. He was subject to the pain and problems which all people face. He never asked us to do that which He was unwilling to do. You can be committed too.

I Can Affirm

The third word in the acrostic is affirmation. There is a power in affirming something that is found nowhere else. There has always been power in affirmation. The Bible says again and again that God spoke this world into existence. The detailed procedure is found in the first chapter of Genesis. There it says repeatedly, "And God said . . .", and things began to happen! And God said, "Let there be light, and there was light." Again and again this happened. The writer declares, "By the word of the Lord were the heavens made. . . .

"For he spoke, and it was done . . ." (Psalms 33:69).

Jesus affirmed or declared what He was going to do,

and He did it. He told of His coming death and sacrifice for the sins of men. He told of His resurrection from the dead. What He said came true.

But you say, *"He was the Son of God."* True! *"We don't have that power."* True! But there is power in saying something aloud. You do not get everything you say, but saying aids the receiving.

Elvis Presley declared that he would die at age forty-three. His mother died at age forty-three. Elvis had a morbid fear of death. He repeated again and again, "I will die at age forty-three." How old was Elvis when he died? Forty-three! *"Just a coincidence,"* you say. *"He died because of an overdose of drugs!"* Yes, but he predicted the year. Is it possible that he programmed himself for death at an early age? I think so.

Here is another thought on what you say. If what others say to us has an influence on our thinking and actions, why wouldn't what we say to ourselves have an influence also?

We know that "the seed of the kingdom is the word of God" (Luke 8). That seed is planted in the heart of man, and the process is begun which results in a new person—a child of God. The word of God is likened to a seed. As we and others plant the words of God in our own hearts, we will grow as followers of Christ should. Then what we say will have an effect on how we live.

Did it make any difference that the prodigal son said, "I will arise and go to my father, and will say unto him, Father, I have sinned against heaven, and before thee, and am no more worthy to be called thy son; make me as one of the hired servants" (Luke 15:18,19)? I believe it did, because the next verse says that he arose and came to his father.

An affirmation is a powerful tool in our hands. When former Cincinnati Reds catcher Johnny Bench was eight years old, he said, "I am going to be the greatest baseball catcher that ever lived." When he graduated from high school, he said the same thing. The records tell the rest of the story.

When Mark Spitz was fifteen years old, he said he was going to win seven Olympic gold medals in swimming. He failed. He only won two! He didn't stop saying it, and four years later he won seven medals and set seven world records. Mark's father told him, "God wants you to be a winner! God didn't make you to be a cursing, sniveling, self–excusing, rationalizing failure. He didn't make you that way!" Did it make any difference what Mark and his father said? I believe it did.

Does this mean that you get everything you say? No, but it means that what you say assists you in getting what you want. Saying it firms the concept in your mind and heart.

Therefore, I challenge you to decide what you want in life and begin asking God for it. He has promised, "Ask, and it shall be given unto you" (Matt. 7:7).

I am not naive enough to suggest that all you have to do to get something is to say it. There is no power in saying alone. But saying and getting started doing it—that's something else! And this brings us to our next word in the acrostic, I CAN.

I Can Never Give Up

The last letter is "N," which stands for *never give up.* Winston Churchill once told a graduating class these words, "Never give up!" Then he sat down. That was all he said. Do you remember what was said at your graduation? I spoke at my graduation, but I don't remember what I said. I wish I had said what he said. They would have remembered it, and I would have remembered it. Therefore, don't quit, don't give up— stick to it!

27

Job of Old Testament fame was a father, a husband, a wealthy man, and a healthy man. He lost all but his life and his wife. His wife looked upon him in his misery and said, ". . . Curse God, and die!" Job replied, ". . . The Lord gave, and the Lord hath taken away; Blessed be the name of the Lord" (Job 1:21). He never gave up, and the Lord blessed him with more children and even greater wealth. Never give up!

Paul of New Testament fame was beaten five times with thirty-nine whip lashes, was beaten with sticks three times, was stoned with rocks, and was shipwrecked three times.

(After that first time, I probably would have said, "I'll never sail again.") He did without food or drink (something I have never done), and was maligned in more than one church (I might have quit preaching long ago). When he wrote his last will and testament to the young preacher Timothy, he included these words, "I have fought a good fight, I have finished my course, I have kept the faith" (II Timothy 4:7). Paul had never quit! He never gave up!

She had polio as a child and had to wear leg braces for six years. The only reason she made the basketball team was because her sister was an outstanding player, and her father would not permit her sister to play without taking her along. She spent most of her time on the bench.

She was six feet tall and weighed eighty-nine pounds when she decided she wanted to be a world-class athlete. She practiced and practiced and practiced. She improved. A college coach noticed her and asked her if she wanted to practice track with his college team. The rest is history. She became the first woman ever to win three gold medals in track and field. She also set three world records. Wilma Rudolph never gave up!

But this is not all of the story. When she went to Tennessee State, there were no athletic scholarships for women. She had to work to pay her way. She worked, she studied, and she practiced track for four years. It was not easy, but she never gave up.

All of us have a power. We might not win any gold medals. We might not become major league baseball players. We might not be martyrs for God. But we can be more than we are. I like the expression, "I ain't what I ought to be, I ain't what I'm going to be, but by the grace of God I ain't what I used to be." Therefore, dream a dream, tell a dream, and do something about that dream. Dreams do come true! You can become!

THINK ABOUT IT

1. What are some of the positive affirmations by individuals in the Bible?
2. What are some word pictures Jesus drew to increase the faith of His disciples?
3. How do you visualize the creation of all things, and what part did the Son of God play in it?
4. What objects which you can see from where you are seated exist because somebody thought about them first?
5. What person in your life is the greatest example of the "never give up" philosophy?
6. What affirmation did Ruth make which brought her a godly husband and prosperity?

CHAPTER 3

POWER TO CONTEMPLATE

She awakened her husband from peaceful slumber to tell him that she heard a noise downstairs in their home. Trying to reassure her, he trudged downstairs only to find himself staring down the barrel of a pistol. The robber demanded that the husband hold his hands up. "Nobody will get hurt," the intruder said, "if you hand over all your valuables and don't cause any trouble."

The man assured the burglar that there would be no outcry and that he was welcome to the silver. "However," he said, "I wish you would do one favor before you go. Go upstairs and meet my wife. She has been looking for you every night for over twenty years."

The *power* of contemplation, reflection, pondering, meditating, or deliberating, is *powerful* indeed. It can be used to produce worry, and it can also be used to produce faith.

Jesus tells a story of an unjust judge. He didn't fear God, and he didn't care what people thought about him. A widow came to him and asked for justice in her dealings with someone. He refused. She came back again. He refused. She came back again. He didn't want to help her. But he did. Why? Because she was on his mind and he couldn't rest until he got her off his mind. He granted her wish (Luke 18:1-8).

Why am I relating this story? Because it points out

the power of contemplation. He couldn't get her off his mind, because she came back again and again and planted the same thought in his mind. He didn't like it. He didn't want it. But there it was. And he went into action because of it.

Why do you buy what you buy when you go to the supermarket? Because your parents bought it before you and programmed your mind for it? Because your neighbor or friend recommended it to you several times? Because you saw it advertised on TV or heard it on radio? Does advertising do any good? You bet it does, or companies wouldn't put millions into it!

If a thirty-second commercial, by repeated viewing, can sell you a product, then isn't it possible for a thirty-minute soap opera, by repeated viewing, to sell you a life-style? Something to think about!

Think About It and You Can Do It

For several years Doug Hooper worked with prisoners in Folsom and San Quentin prisons on the West Coast. In *You Are What You Think* he tells this story.

"I doubt if there is any one group of people anywhere who feel that they have less control over their lives than men in prison. Their whole lives are regimented, except for one thing: they still have control over their thoughts, and the way they react to situations.

"First, let me explain about Folsom Prison. It is called the 'end of the line.' When a man finally reaches Folsom, it generally means that everything has been tried and failed. He's had therapy, psychiatry, and whatever else the system had to offer.

"Ten years ago I had an interview with their warden asking if I could start a monthly class on a volunteer basis. I felt I could help the men develop a better attitude and self image.

"The warden was very pessimistic. 'These men don't

have the slightest desire to improve themselves,' he said. 'You will be just wasting your time.'

"I was confident I could prove him wrong. Not because of me, but because the principles I would be teaching them are absolutely infallible. They are natural laws, and work regardless of race, creed, financial condition, age, or sex.

"I was challenging the men to produce a circumstance that couldn't be changed. A big fellow named Joe stood up. Joe had been in prison for the better part of twenty years. Much of that time had been spent in solitary confinement.

"Joe was somewhat belligerent when he said, 'I've got a circumstance that can't be changed by any change of thinking or attitude.' He went on to explain that he had an early morning job in the mess hall. He was awakened at 4 A.M., and escorted by a very surly guard to help with the breakfast crew. This guard would come in cursing loudly and rattling his keys, purposely awakening the whole cell block. Joe hated this man so much, it was making him a nervous wreck. 'The only way I can change this situation is to hit him over the head, which is exactly what I am going to do someday!'

"I could tell by the way he said it that this wasn't very far off. I said, 'All right, but let's try something else first.'

"I shocked him by telling him to feel sorry for the guard. I explained what a miserable, unhappy person he must be, or he wouldn't act the way he did. Then I suggested to Joe that the next morning when the guard came around, he should say 'good morning' to him.

"On my next visit, Joe was there with a big grin on his face. It was the first time I had ever seen him smile. He stood up and told his story to the group. 'I laid awake all that night wondering how I was going to say good morning to that . . .,' he said. 'But I managed to grunt it out. I stopped him cold! The next morning he came in quietly, and we grunted good morning to each other. The third morning we started talking, and found we had a mutual interest in fishing and hunting. Since then, we have become friends, and he has changed his attitude toward others and is becoming well liked.'

"Even if the guard hadn't changed, it wouldn't have mattered as far as Joe was concerned. The situation lost its power over him the minute he changed his mind about it!

"Joe changed so completely after this incident that he was released much sooner than he had previously dared to hope. He wrote me that it had given him such a wonderful feeling to know that he had the power within himself to handle any situation that might come along simply by controlling his thoughts and his attitudes."

There is one statement in this story that I want you to examine. Joe said, "I laid awake all that night wondering how I was going to say good morning. . . ." This statement magnifies the power of contemplation. He had pondered how he was going to say a simple "good morning," and uttering those words was the changing point in his life.

Perhaps you have an encounter scheduled for tomorrow. You don't know what's going to happen. Perhaps it is with your boss. Maybe it is with an in-law. Maybe you are facing someone to whom you owe a debt. See yourself being calm and relaxed as you listen and comment. Decide now that you are going to maintain poise and confidence, regardless of how the other person acts. Visualize a peaceful encounter and expect it. Think about it. You have everything to gain and nothing to lose. You are in control!

The Mother of Jesus Was a Master of Contemplation

The angel announced the birth of Christ to the shepherds. They made the sayings known to Mary and Joseph and others. Some wondered, but "Mary kept all these things, and pondered them in her heart" (Luke 2:19).

When they found Jesus conversing with the doctors in the temple after a three-day search, Jesus said to Mary and Joseph, "How is it that you sought me? Know you not that I must be about my Father's business?" They didn't understand that saying. "And he went down with them, and came to Nazareth, and was subject to them: but his mother kept all these sayings in her heart" (Luke 2:49-51).

Eighteen years passed. "And the third day there was a marriage in Cana of Galilee; and the mother of Jesus was there: and both Jesus was called, and his disciples, to the marriage. And when they wanted wine, the mother of Jesus said unto him, 'They have no wine.' Jesus said to her, 'Woman, what have I to do with thee? Mine hour is not yet come'" (John 2:1-4).

Why did Mary speak to Jesus when they were out of wine? He was not in the vineyard business. They were not at their home, where wine might have been stored. He had never performed a miracle in her presence. This was to be His first. Why? Because she knew who He was. Because she knew He could help if He wanted to.

But He rejected her suggestion. Was she crushed? Was she disappointed? How did she react? She calmly said to the servants, "Whatsoever he says to you, do it" (John 2:5).

How could she do this? Had He not told her to bother Him no more? What had happened in her past that prepared her for this great miracle?

For thirty years she had been contemplating what the shepherds had said about Jesus. For eighteen years she had been meditating upon what had happened in the temple. She had kept all His sayings in her heart. These seed thoughts were churning and turning in her mind, and now the time to act upon them was come. "Out of the abundance of the heart the mouth speaks."

All of these thoughts were creating faith in her heart—faith which led her to act even when she seemingly had been rejected by her own son. This is the power of contemplation.

What you think about determines what you say. What you reflect upon determines what you do. It will make the difference between success and defeat.

Set Your Mind on Healthy Thoughts

The Bible talks about sound doctrine. Sound teaching is healthy teaching—teaching that will build us up for service to others.

How do you keep evil thoughts from living in the bedroom of your mind? Do you put out a sign which says "No Rooms Available," or do you fill up those rooms with other occupants?

Some people clean up their acts and feel that this is sufficient. Jesus said that it is not enough. "When the unclean spirit is gone out of a man, he walks through dry places, seeking rest; and finding none, he says, I will return unto my house where I came out. And when he comes, he finds it swept and orderly. Then he goes and takes seven other spirits more wicked than himself; and they enter in and dwell there: and the last state of that man is worse than the first" (Luke 11:24-26). A broom is not weapon enough to keep out the devil!

You cannot think two things at the same time. Therefore, you must think either healthy thoughts or unhealthy thoughts. A person does not think healthy thoughts all the time, but he can set his mind on healthy and wholesome thoughts. By so doing, he fills up the rooms of his mind with tenants who will help him rather than hinder him.

The Bible talks about mindset or setting your mind. We know how to set a clock. This relieves our mind and reduces anxiety. We know how to set a table. Read a book by Amy Vanderbilt or some other authority on etiquette. We know how to set a watch. Find an exact and authoritative time.

Some people have their minds "set on earthly things" (Philippians 3:19). You can "set your mind on things above" (Colossians 3:2). What does this mean? One translation says to "think about" or contemplate.

Before Paul affirmed, "I can do all things through Christ who strengthens me," he said, "Replace anxiety with prayer and thanksgiving, and the peace of God shall keep or guard your hearts and minds through Christ Jesus" (Philippians 4:6,7).

His climactic *close* to those thoughts is this: "Finally, brethren, whatsoever things are true, whatsoever things are honest, whatsoever things are just, whatsoever things are pure, whatsoever things are lovely, whatsoever things are of good report, if there be any virtue, and if there be any praise, think on these things." One translation says to "fill your mind with those things that are good. . . ."

What do you think about? What do you keep in your heart? If you keep anger and hurt in your heart, what will you reap? If you keep faith and hope in your heart, you will enjoy the harvest much more.

S. C. Boyce is a teacher at David Lipscomb College. He said that a professional bum was asked, "Why have you led a 'bum' life?" The quick reply was this: "Because I thought 'bum' thoughts."

What do you want to be? Think about it, and that's
what you will become.

THINK ABOUT IT

1. What is one thing you have thought about at least once
   each day for a month? How has this contemplation influenced you?
2. Write down what you think about most during a one-
   hour period of your life during one day this week.
3. What process would you follow to replace unhealthy
   thoughts? Compare the procedure of maintaining good
   physical health with the process of maintaining good
   spiritual health.
4. Explore the possibilities of why Jesus changed the
   water into wine after rejecting Mary's suggestion.
5. If Mary planted the seed thought in the mind of Jesus
   which motivated Him to perform His first miracle,
   would this be the first time mortals have influenced
   deity? If not, what are some other examples?

CHAPTER 4

POWER TO CHANGE

A penetrating letter came to my desk recently. The writer captured my attention with these words: "Presently, I feel my life and personal fellowship with Christ are out of control. I'm out of control with anger, complaining constantly with my wife and children. . . . I'm forever finding fault, particularly in my twelve-year-old who has had cancer but is now in remission. When he was so ill, I spoiled him terribly, and I don't know how to control my feelings of anger toward him. . . . I'm out of control. . . . I have never in my life been so greedy for food and attention. It's sickening, and I hate it. I've turned quite selfish and extremely impatient. I'm not consistent in my walk with the Lord. I don't think of others. I don't have a forgiving spirit. Nor do I ever listen to my wife and children or God. . . . Please help me; I'm out of control."

This is only part of the letter. There is more, and all of it is negative and discouraging. There are several disturbing things about this letter. First of all, the writer had nothing good to say about himself. Second, it was written over a month before I received it. Third, it was mimeographed. This gentleman had made several copies of this letter to send out to several people who might be able to help. This indicated that he did not feel that his problems were going to go away overnight.

I answered his letter and sent some materials which he requested. He wrote another letter, and this letter was more encouraging. The material that impressed him most was a tract by Jack Exum entitled, "How Do You Know You Are Accepted When You Fail and Don't Do Good?"

This letter and his response to my letter magnifies what I have believed for a long time. A major problem of mankind is a low self–image. Wouldn't this be a wonderful world if everyone would arise in the morning and say, "This is the day which the Lord has made. I will rejoice and be glad in it?"

But you say, *"I don't feel like rejoicing when I get up in the morning."* True! You might not feel like going to work, but you go anyway, right? The world would come to a standstill if everyone did just what he felt like doing. It would be disaster! It has been said that we act our way into feeling, not feel our way into acting. Therefore, arise and say it anyway! You'll be glad you did.

"But I can't change!" You are right. As long as you say that, you are right. I never said it would be easy to change. But it is worth it.

A factory worker was complaining to his partner on the job. "Peanut butter and jelly sandwiches and apples! Apple and peanut butter sandwich! Every day, day in and day out, same old thing! I'm getting sick and tired of peanut butter and jelly and apples."

His friend suggested, "Why don't you get your wife to prepare something else?"

"I can't. I'm not married! I prepare my own lunch." You might think this is a joke, but I told this story recently, and a gentleman exclaimed, "I'm the man!" Another factory worker said, "I have worked with a man for twenty years, and everyday at lunch he eats an egg salad sandwich." It is not easy to change, but it can be done.

I'm Too Old to Change

"You can't teach an old dog new tricks." First of all, you are not a dog. Second, we are not talking about tricks which will entertain folks around you. We are talking about changes that will bless your life, bring you happiness, and bring happiness to others. The real question is not how old you are, but whether you really want to change.

When Jesus approached the man who had been sick for thirty-eight years, He asked the question, "Do you want to get well?" His answer indicated that he did, and Jesus healed him (John 5). What if he had said no? Jesus never forced Himself on anyone.

I am glad that one verse in the Bible is designed especially for older folks. The apostle Peter was explaining the phenomenon of speaking in different languages when he said, "This is that which was spoken by the prophet Joel. 'And it shall come to pass in the last days,' says God, 'I will pour out my Spirit upon all flesh: and your sons and your daughters shall prophesy, and your men shall see visions, and your old men shall dream dreams: . . .'" (Acts 2:17,18).

God was actually going to use old men in His plans to bring people back to Him. The company might have put you on the shelf at sixty-five, but God says, "I can use you!"

Two men were visiting a lady to talk about the new book which she had written. She was ninety-three. She didn't want to talk about that book, but about her next book which would be completed in seven years.

"But I might begin a project and not live to complete

it." That doesn't matter! My father planted several pecan trees. Some of them died. While cutting one of them down, he suffered a heart attack and died the next day. He never enjoyed the fruits of his labors, but my mother and his sons have.

Today, you and I are enjoying the creations of generations before us. We are driving on paved roads we did not build and using tools we did not design. We are flying in planes we did not visualize and watching events on television we never dreamed would be possible.

The Bridge Builder

An old man, going a lone highway
Came at the evening, cold and gray,
To a chasm, vast and deep and wide,
Through which was flowing a sullen tide.
The old man crossed in the twilight dim;
The sullen stream had no fears for him:
But he turned when safe on the other side
And built a bridge to span the tide.

"Old man," said the fellow pilgrim near,
"You are wasting strength with building here;
Your journey will end with the ending day;
You never again must pass this way;
You have crossed the chasm, deep and wide—
Why build you the bridge at the eventide?"

The builder lifted his old gray head:
"Good friend, in the path I have come," he said,
"There followeth after me today
A youth whose feet must pass this way.
This chasm that has been naught to me
To that fair-haired youth may a pitfall be

41

He, too, must cross in the twilight dim;
Good friend, I am building the bridge for him."
                              —Will Allen Dromgoole

Every word you say, every smile you smile, every
deed you do will not go unnoticed by those with whom
you work. ". . . Your old . . . shall dream dreams. . . ."
Do it, and joy will be yours!

I Want to Change

"I want to change, but people might criticize me."
Good! Let them criticize!

Coretta King, widow of the late Martin Luther
King, answered the critics who believed blacks were
inferior. "I knew I was not inferior, because nobody ever
goes to such lengths to oppress or to retard a basically
inferior person."

My friend Neil Gallagher says, "Attacks do not come
to garbage dumps, but to jewelry stores." You are not
garbage. You are a diamond!

A politician did the best job he could. He made
mistakes and was criticized severely. The objections
contained grave errors. He visited a friend in the
country and asked his advice. The farmer could scarely
hear the story because his hound dog was barking at
the full moon. The farmer told the dog to stop, but he
kept on howling.

The farmer answered the politician. "You want to
know how to answer the critics. Listen to that dog.
Look at the moon. Remember, people will keep
howling at you. They will snap at you and criticize you.
But here's the answer: The dogs keep howling, but the
moon keeps shining."

Jesus, the best man who ever lived, was criticized.
You will be too.

How Can I Feel Better about Myself

"You have put me in the company with Jesus now. I know that He was great and good, but I am not in the same league." Aren't you? Listen to these words.

"When I consider thy heavens, the work of thy fingers, the moon and the stars, which thou hast ordained; What is man, that thou are mindful of him? and the son of man, that thou visited him? For thou hast made him a little lower than the angels, and hast crowned him with glory and honour. Thou madest him to have dominion over the works of thy hands: thou hast put all things under his feet: all sheep and oxen, yea, and the beast of the field; the fowl of the air, and the fish of the sea, and whatsoever passeth through the paths of the seas. O Lord our Lord, how excellent is thy name in all the earth" (Psalms 8:3-9).

Most of us have been to a zoo where there is a cage with bars. Inside is a trapeze or a tree or both. People are swinging from the limbs, and monkeys are tossing peanuts through the bars to the people who perform. Is that the way it is? Certainly not! A situation like the one in *Planet of the Apes* never has been, is not, and never will be. People are in control! God placed us in charge.

You are different from all of God's other creations. And God said, "Let us make man in our image, after our likeness. . . . So God created man in his own image, in the image of God created he him; male and female created he them" (Genesis 1:26,27). You have an imprint on you that no other of God's creation has. You are different from all other people. Even identical twins are not exactly alike. You are unique. You are valuable. You are to be counted.

You have a value which you had when you were born. You didn't *earn* it, and you didn't *achieve* it. What is

43

more, you can't get rid of it! What is it? Built-in value. I don't care what others say about you. You are valuable! You count for something!

God Loves Everyone Equally

There is a reason why God loves everyone with an equal love. Because of who you are! We love because of achievement, accomplishment, or performance. God loves us regardless of achievement, accomplishment, or performance. We are attracted to people who love us. God loves those who do not love Him. He loves because we are His creation.

Think about this. God does not love you more because you do good things. He does not love you less because you do bad things. His love for you is constant.

This does not mean that you will not prosper when you do good things. This does not mean that you will not suffer when you do bad things. You will reap what you sow. This is a law of God.

There is a story that Jesus tells which demonstrates these truths. It is the story of the prodigal son and the older brother (Luke 15). In the story, the father represents God. The two brothers represent the religious sinner and the prodigal sinner. The father loves the prodigal son just as much when he leaves home as he did when he was on the farm. This is demonstrated by his running to him and kissing him when he sees him coming home. This was done before the son ever confessed his sins.

The older brother is upset because the father throws a party for the wayward son who has returned. The older brother is angry and will not go to the party. There he stands—self-righteous, judgmental, and proud. The father loves him just as much when he shows this ugly attitude as he did when he was working on the farm. In fact, he goes the second mile and comes out to encourage him and plead with him. He accepts him and reassures him. This story demonstrates the great love of God. Again, I reiterate this great maxim: God does not love you more because you do good, and He does not love you less because you do bad things.

What does this do for you when you have a low self-image? What does this do for you when you have failed again and again? What does this do for you when the majority of what you have heard about yourself has been negative?

It helps you to realize that you are created and loved by God. It creates an atmosphere and environment in which you can grow and prosper as a person and as a servant of God. You are valuable! You are important!

Johnny Lingo was a trader in the islands of the Pacific. He was engaged to the chieftain's daughter. In the opinion of the villagers, the chieftain's daughter was no prize. One remarked that she had a face like a stone and looked as if she had missed many meals. She walked with a shuffle and gazed at the ground. She never smiled and scarcely said a word. She cared little about her appearance and her clothes. The people said that Johnny would never come back for her when he went to the mainland and saw all the beautiful women there.

But Johnny did come back. And the meeting to negotiate for the chieftain's daughter was set. All of the villagers were present. The chief had determined that he would ask four cows for his daughter, even though he had a low opinion of her. The standard price for women on the island was three cows.

The bargaining began. The chieftain said, "Four cows!" Johnny responded, "Eight cows!" The people gasped in astonishment. When the chieftain recovered from the shock, he took his eight cows and went on his way rejoicing. Johnny and his bride went away to a neighboring island for the honeymoon.

When Johnny and his bride came back to the home island, people noticed a difference in his young bride. She now walked with a bounce in her step. She held her head erect, smiled, and conversed intelligently. She wore the latest fashions and looked like the daughter of a chief. The chieftain went about the village, complaining about the way Johnny had cheated him in that transaction.

What made the difference? She was the same young lady. She was royalty before she left with her new husband. The difference was evident. She was an "eight cow woman!" A price had been paid for her which had never been paid for any other woman on that island.

When we recognize that God has paid a price for us which no one has ever paid for anyone before, we walk tall, smile, and endure anything this old world has to offer. "God so loved the world that he gave his only begotten son . . ." (John 3:16). God's love motivates us to believe in ourselves, to raise our self-worth and to create within us the power to change.

You can make up your mind. Are you going to accept the appraisal of the world concerning your self-worth, or are you going to accept the testimony of God? The decision is yours.

A lady had guilt feelings about her past. She had not forgiven herself. A counselor suggested that she visualize herself finding a gold mine under a garbage dump. She envisions herself going to the bank to borrow money to buy that garbage dump. She cannot tell the banker about the gold mine because he might purchase it before she has a chance to do so.

The counselor then remarked, "You see something valuable which the banker does not see. He sees a garbage dump, but you see a gold mine. This is the way

God looks at you. You see a garbage dump, but he sees a gold mine underneath!"

Begin now to look for gold in your life and not garbage. You can change! You will change! How? "I can do all things through Christ who strengthens me" (Philippians 4:13).

POWER TO CHANGE

1. When God made man, what instructions did He give which established man's power to change?
2. What statement did God make to Cain, the brother of Abel, which showed he had the power to change the direction of his life?
3. What is the nature of repentance, the message of the prophets and the Old Testament worthies?
4. What is the nature of the gospel of Jesus Christ?
5. Relate a specific incident in your life where you made a change. What was the major motivation which brought about this change?
6. Does heredity have an influence on the direction of our lives? Discuss Ezekiel, chapter 18, with heredity in view.
7. Relate an incident in your life when you were counted valuable, even when you did the wrong thing.
8. How could you demonstrate "Hosea-type" love for someone who has disappointed you in life?

CHAPTER 5

POWER TO START

Jesus concluded His sermon on the mount with these words, "Not everyone that saith unto me, Lord, Lord, shall enter into the kingdom of heaven: but he that doeth the will of my Father which is in heaven . . ." (Matt. 7:21). Jesus concluded His sermons to His disciples before He went to the cross with these words: "Inasmuch as you have done it unto one of the least of these my brethren, you have done it unto me" (Matt. 25:40).

Do and *done* are key words in the vocabulary of our Lord. The big question is, "How do we get started doing the things we know we need to be doing anyway?"

Robert Schuller has said that the most important thing he learned at Hope College in Michigan was from a coach who taught History 101. None of the students had started their term papers in the middle of the semester. The coach said that he didn't care if they finished the course, but he wanted them to remember this one sentence which he shouted, "Beginning is half done!"

The key word is *beginning*. Everyone has to start somewhere. How did you get started reading this book? It happened because you learned to read at one time in your past. It didn't happen all at once.

University of Tennessee football coach Johnny Majors came home from his first day at school looking depressed and dejected. His mother said, "What's the matter, Johnny?" "No need for me to go to school anymore, Mom," he replied. "Why, Johnny." "I can't even read," was his sad response. Everyone has to learn to read, and it doesn't happen overnight. First you learn an "A" and a "B," then a word, then two. But it happens only when you begin!

You Have Already Begun

You are on your way to doing some of the things you want to do. How do I know? Because you have experience. *"What do you mean, experience?"* I mean that you have cultivated growth habits in your life that will enable you to do what you want to do now.

For example, do you drive a car? How did you get started driving? Did you wake up one morning, go to the garage, back the car out of the garage, and drive down the street all by yourself? I think not! You were taught to drive a car. Your parents or a friend or a driving instructor at school taught you the fundamentals. Each day you gained confidence, and now you drive an automobile automatically. You don't get in the car and say to yourself, "Now, what do I do next?" Driving comes automatically.

How did you learn to cook? You watched your mother or your grandmother. You learned from the home economics teacher at school. Perhaps you took a course in cooking. The ability to cook did not come down from heaven miraculously. It was a learned experience.

Are you a mechanic? You must have learned from a "shade-tree mechanic"—perhaps your father, grandfather, or a friend. Perhaps you had a job at the local service station or you went to mechanics school.

Are you a teacher? Did you graduate from high

school, walk into the principal's office, smile, and offer your services as a professor in that institution? We know better, don't we? The response would have been, "Come back in four or five years and we'll talk about it!" You learned from other teachers, attended college, met the requirements, and then were ready to teach in the school system. Practice, practice, practice made you efficient in what you are now doing.

A famous pianist was once complimented with this wish, "I'd give half my life to play like you do." "That's exactly what it cost me," was his abrupt reply.

You have the raw materials from which the finished product can be developed and used. You know this, because there are many things you have already learned to do. Now let's move on to new adventures in growing.

You Have the Power To Start

"Well, I know what I want to do with my life. I want to be a better servant of God. I want to study the Bible more. I want to pray more. I want to share the message of Christ with others."

That's good. I compliment your ambition and zeal. You have goals. You have to progress. Here is a very simple suggestion which will help you to reach your goals.

Several years ago I had back problems. A doctor told me that walking a mile each day would help strengthen my back. I began to walk daily. I noticed that my right foot was hurting, and this was discouraging to me. I didn't know what to do. Through the encouragement of my wife, I saw a physical therapist in Dallas, Texas. He asked me to walk across the room and stand before him. "Did you never notice that when you stand, your right foot is spread wider than your left?" he queried. "I hadn't noticed that," was my reply.

"I suggest that you walk and concentrate on holding your right foot parallel to your left when you walk," was his sound advice. I did this for the next several weeks. It became a habit. Now I walk properly without thinking about it. I have no pain in my foot.

Isn't it amazing what a slight adjustment can do to help you? I am going to suggest a slight adjustment to the goals you have set. Instead of saying, *"I want to become a better servant of God,"* say, *"I will say a kind word to someone every day."* Instead of saying, *"I want to pray more,"* say, *"I will pray each morning at 6:30."* Instead of saying, *"I want to share the message of Christ with others,"* say, *"I will talk to a shut-in once every week."*

You Can Set Specific Goals

What's the difference? The difference is that you are setting specific goals instead of general goals. You have placed a time limit on your goals, and you have talked about doing a specific deed.

A farmer was once asked how he plowed a row so straight. "I just drive a stake down on the other side of the field and plow straight to it." That is the way to set goals. Know where you are going. Make it specific, and set a time limit on it.

What I am about to say might well be the most important statement in this book. Are you ready? Here it is. WRITE IT DOWN! That's right, write it down! Decide what you want—your specific goal—and write it down. What difference could writing it down make?

Andy Daniels was a student in Dickson where I had just begun ministering. On Sunday evening I was asked to select someone for the dismissal prayer. I asked Andy. He said he would be happy to do it. He led a fine prayer. After the services, one of the elders called me aside and said, "Did you know Andy is not a member of the church?" I said, "No, I didn't know that."

Monday morning, I wrote a letter to Andy encouraging him to become a Christian. I enclosed a booklet which I had written, entitled *Don't Die on Third*. I knew Andy liked sports, and the booklet contained a message on life drawn from the game of baseball. I received a letter from Andy the following week. He had been baptized! He wrote "Your letter and the booklet *Don't Die on Third* caused me to take the final steps."

There is power in writing. How many times have you received a letter which lifted your spirit and caused a great change to take place in your life?

Recently I asked Jim Bill McInteer, respected minister in the church of Christ, to write a letter of recommendation for me. He did this in glowing terms. Anytime I feel a spirit of depression hovering over me, I can read that letter and have my spirit lifted.

Can you believe this? After writing this beautiful letter about me and my wife, Ruth, he wrote in another letter: "Thank you for letting me write you a letter of recommendation." This took my breath! He was thanking me for letting him do me a favor! Do I believe there is power in writing? I am a believer!

Several years ago I met a couple in Ohio who had moved here from Europe. They were learning English by studying the Bible. They were convinced by the word of God and wanted to be baptized, but didn't know whom to contact. Therefore, the husband baptized his wife in the bathtub, and she rendered the same service for him immediately. Eventually, they came in contact with the church of Christ there and were meeting with them faithfully at the last report. There is power in the written word!

God called His servant John to write these words,

"And many other signs truly did Jesus in the presence of his disciples, which are not written in this book: But these are written, that you might believe that Jesus is the Christ, the Son of God; and that believing, you might have life through his name" (John 20:30,31).

God not only commissioned John to write the story of the life of Jesus on earth, but he selected three other men to do the same—Matthew, Mark, and Luke.

The greatest document of the greatest life which has ever been lived has been written. Jesus said on numerous occasions, "It is written . . . ." There is power in the written word of God!

That same power is available to sustain our belief, as well as to create it. "These things have I written unto you that believe on the name of the Son of God: that you may know that you have eternal life, and that you may believe on the name of the Son of God" (I John 5:13).

Why did John write? So believers could know that they have life, that they might be confident as they continue in this faith which they have in Jesus! The greatest life is the life which is eternal. The written word sustains and continues to build up that faith.

Abraham Lincoln was influenced tremendously by that which was written. In *Abraham Lincoln: The Man and His Faith* G. Frederick Owen tells of nine books which entered Lincoln's life in his youth: "the Bible, to teach him of God and moral responsibility; *Pilgrim's Progress,* to stimulate his motives to one day reach Heaven; *The Life of Washington,* to teach him love for and loyalty to his country; and *Aesop's Fables,* from which he learned shrewdness and humor and the value of a story . . ." (page 9). The other five were: *Webster's Speller, Robinson Crusoe, The Arabian Nights, The Life of Benjamin Franklin,* and *History of the United States.* As you read about Lincoln, can you not see the power of the written word in his remarkable life?

Benjamin Franklin said that he owed much of his

success and happiness to a certain method of learning. What was it? Early in his career, he found himself heavily in debt. He looked for a method to help. That method was the writing down of thirteen principles and determining to master them, one at a time. He would work enthusiastically on one of them for a week, and then go on to the next one. When he finished the thirteen, he would start all over again. There is power in setting goals and writing them down.

Write It Down and Do It Now

Write down one specific goal which you really want. If you do not have a burning desire for a new goal now, ask God to help you find the goal which will help you and glorify Him. He says, "Ask, and you shall receive."

Read this goal aloud every day. Carry it with you in your automobile. Put it on your sun visor. Tape it on your mirror in the bathroom. Put it in front of your Bible. Fasten it on your refrigerator. Put it on the bedside table. Leave it by the telephone. Each morning and each evening, say it aloud.

What did Moses tell the children of Israel? "Hear O Israel: The Lord our God is one Lord: And thou shalt love the Lord thy God with all thine heart, and with all thy soul, and with all thy might. And these words, which I command you this day, shall be in your heart: And thou shalt teach them diligently unto thy children, and shalt talk of them when thou sittest in thine house, and when thou walkest by the way, and when thou liest down, and when thou risest up. And thou shalt bind them for a sign upon thine hand, and they shall be as frontlets between thine eyes. And thou shalt write them upon the posts of thy house, and on thy gates" (Deuteronomy 6:4-9).

This was God's program for developing His people.

Again and again, they were to teach, listen, read, and write the goals they were to accomplish.

Write it down, read it aloud, talk about it. This is God's plan. Can we improve on it? It is a good plan, and we encourage you to begin now to put it into action. You can do it! Get started on your specific goal now.

POWER TO START

1. Analyze the most fulfilling project you ever worked on and how you got started doing it.
2. What is one challenge you have always had a desire to tackle? Decide on the first step you will have to take to get started doing it.
3. Tell of a letter or printed message you have received which brought happiness or change of direction to your life.
4. What books other than the Bible have assisted you in your spiritual growth?
5. Write down one specific goal you want and say it aloud every morning and every night for the next twenty-one days. If you do not have a specific goal, then write these words: The date is (today). I am beginning my search for a specific goal. I am excited about it!

CHAPTER 6

POWER TO FINISH

A friend of mine tells this story about his boyhood. He entered a race and was running well ahead of the others. His confidence was high until someone accelerated past him as if he were standing still. He was so discouraged he dropped out of the race. When the winner was announced, he learned that the young man who passed him had been disqualified because of his age. If he had only stayed in the race, he would have won. But it was too late.

Beginning is having a project half-done, but the challenges come in running the race. You have begun to set goals. You have written them down. You are saying them aloud each morning and each night. Congratulations!

Anticipate things happening to offset your goals. For example, you want to pray each morning at 6:30, but your child gets sick. You want to read your Bible each evening at 9:30, but you have company. You want to say a kind word to someone every day, but you never get out of the house to see anyone. You want to walk a mile every day, but it has been raining all day long. You have a goal up on the bathroom mirror, but your mate makes fun of it. "You can't do that." "You've never done that before." "Who do you think you are?" "You've tried that before and failed." Do these sentences sound familiar? They should, because they are spoken not only by your enemies, but by your friends.

Remember when Jesus told His disciples what He was going to do—go to Jerusalem, suffer, and finally be killed? Peter said, "Lord, this shall not be." Jesus responded, "Get thee behind me, Satan . . ." (Matthew 16:23). Was Jesus saying that Peter was Satan? No. But He was saying that the response of Peter was the response of the devil.

This passage teaches that even the best of people can say things which are of the devil, even when they mean well. Peter probably thought that the Lord was depressed. Therefore, he would cheer him up. But Peter did not understand the goal of Jesus.

People do not understand your goal. Therefore, they say things that discourage, rather than encourage. Perhaps they want to see you escape the pain of failure. They mean well, but what they say does not build you up.

Perhaps you have already failed to meet your goal many times. This does not mean that you have ultimately failed. There is a difference between failure and temporary defeat. The person who fails is the person who does not meet his goal and quits. Temporary defeat is different. Maybe you did not meet your goal today. Tomorrow is another day. You can do it tomorrow. Tomorrow was another day for Peter, and he did not quit.

The Lord told Peter that he was going to fail three times, but He provided an atmosphere in which Peter could grow, even when he was failing. He said, "Simon, Simon, behold, Satan has desire to have you . . . but I have prayed for you, that your faith fail not: and when you are converted, strengthen your brethren" (Luke 22:31,32). If Jesus could give Peter room to grow, you can give yourself room to grow!

When you learned to walk, did your parents tell you,

"Three chances are all you receive; then it's back in the playpen for you?" Certainly not! Over and over again you tried to walk, and then one day it happened. Today you are growing in your goals. So what if you fall down. Get up and do it again.

You Can Try Ten Thousand Times

Thomas Edison conducted over ten thousand experiments before he became successful in producing electricity in a bulb. He was asked if he wanted to quit. He replied, "No, I have learned ten thousand ways it will not work. I know I am getting close to success, because I have tried most of the ways that will not work." What an attitude!

Jesus talked about forgiveness which staggers the human imagination: "seventy times seven" and "seven times in one day." No wonder the disciples replied, "Increase our faith" (Luke 17). God would not ask us to forgive our fellow man seven times in the same day if He were not willing to do the same! Can we not allow ourselves some mistakes as we grow in our goals? Absolutely!

There are people who make a million dollars a year and meet temporary defeat seven out of every ten times they try. In the world of baseball, a few can make an out seven out of every ten times they go to the bat. We call it success! How do they handle those temporary defeats?

Here is the way Babe Ruth expressed it. On one occasion in Philadelphia, he had struck out three times. Each time the crowd booed, Ruth would go back to the dugout, tip his hat to the crowd, smile, and sit down. On his last trip to the plate, he had two strikes, and then hit the ball, not into the stands, but completely out of the ball park. The crowd cheered as he came back to the dugout. He tipped his hat, smiled, and sat down.

He was asked by a sportswriter, "Babe, how is it that you act the same when you strike out as when you hit a home run?" He replied, "I know the law of averages is working for me. If I keep on swinging, sooner or later I am going to connect."

By the way, do you know who held the record for strike-outs in the major leagues until recently? You guessed it! Babe Ruth. He hit the most home runs in his time, but he also broke the record for most strike-outs. Maybe you have struck out many times, but you have some home runs stored up in you too. Keep on swinging!

"But it hurts to strike out!" "It hurts to fall down!" I know, but failing is a part of growing and achieving.

A little boy was leading his sister up a mountain path, and the trail was rather difficult. The little girl complained, "Why, this isn't a path at all! It's rocky and bumpy!" And her brother replied, "Sure, the bumps are what you climb on."

One day Charlie Brown was complaining because his team always lost their games. Lucy tried hard to console him by saying, "Remember, Charlie Brown, you learn more from your defeats than your victories." Charlie Brown replied, "That makes me the smartest man in the world!"

There is no gain without pain. There is no success without defeat. There is no growth without stretching. Don't quit! Winners never quit, and quitters never win!

Ray Kroc said, "Press on: Nothing in the world can take the place of persistence. Talent will not: nothing is more common than unsuccessful individuals with talent. Genius will not: unrewarded genius is almost a proverb. Education will not: the world is full of educated derelicts. Persistence and determination alone are omnipotent" (*Seeds of Greatness,* Simon and Schuster, Inc., page 126).

You Can Do It One Day at a Time

How do you eat an elephant? One bite at a time! I don't relish the meals, but it could be done over a period of weeks, months, and years. This is the way progress is made—one step at a time. A football player does not quit because he doesn't make a touchdown every time he gets the ball. The best of players is thrown for a loss. What do they do? They get up and carry the ball again. Very few times is a ball carried for seventy or eighty yards at a time. Usually the gains are a few steps at a time. Ira North was once asked, "How many more do you want at Madison?" "Just one more," was his enthusiastic response.

Remember when you learned to type? The instructor told you to put your fingers on the home keys— asdf, jkl;. *"But that doesn't spell anything. I want to learn to make words!"* But you have to start somewhere, and these letters are home base for the typist. Then the teacher asked you to look at the chart on the wall. *"What? I can't look at my fingers? Why, I could lose my little finger when it gets stuck in the keys?"* Patience, patience. You do it and you do it and you do it over and over again. Eureka! You can type! The words begin to come easily. Today you can fairly fly over the keyboard.

Jesus talked about the importance of daily exercises. "Give us this day our daily bread." "Do not worry about tomorrow. . . . Each day has enough trouble of its own" (Matthew 6:34). "If any man will come after me, let him deny himself, and take up his cross daily, and follow me" (Luke 9:23).

Exercise your goal every day for twenty-one days, and it will become a habit. When a football player is handed the ball, he doesn't pause and think, "Now what I am going to do with it?" When a typist is handed a piece of paper, she doesn't hesitate, but places it in the machine and begins to type. When the instructor tells you to take notes, you take pen in hand and begin to write. Why? Because you acquired the habit years and years ago. Now you are developing new habits which will be with you for years to come. You can do it one day at a time!

You Can Learn from a Minnesota Pike

A Minnesota pike was deposited in a large fish tank. Minnows were dropped into the water. He began to gobble them up. Then minnows were dropped into a glass cylinder which had been lowered into the water. When the pike approached them, he would bump his nose on the cylinder. Soon he grew weary of trying. The bottomless glass cylinder was lifted, and the minnows swam freely around him, bumping into his sides and nose. He made no effort to eat them. He **literally** died in a tank of food. Why? Because he did not believe that he could do it. Because he quit an hour too soon!

Don't quit now! Perhaps you have set your goals too high. It is very important that we set realistic and easy-to-reach goals at first.

For example, your goal is to teach a friend about Christ. How about a short-range goal with a view to teaching him about Jesis? "I will listen to my friend more than I talk to him today" could be a short-range goal. "I will pray for my friend every day." "I will ask questions which identify his felt need." "I will compliment him one time today."

A customer was determined that he was going to

61

compliment a grouchy, unfriendly postal clerk. He searched diligently and presented this pleasing remark: "I wish I had your head of hair." The clerk smiled and changed almost instantly.

Perhaps your goal is to build up the temple of God—your body—by walking five miles every day. How much do you walk now? *"Oh, just a little at my work."* Set a short-range goal to walk one block. You could set a goal to do fifty push-ups, then do forty, and not reach your goal. Why not set a goal to do one push-up each day? You say, *"That's not much!"* How many are you doing now? *"Oh, not any!"* Do one, and then increase the number gradually. These successes will encourage you to keep on and not quit. It might look good to set a large goal, but whom are you trying to impress? A big target is easier for your critics to hit when you meet with temporary defeat.

Be a Turtle and not a Squirrel

I live in the Middle Tennessee foothills, the home of squirrels and turtles. While driving down the road, I have observed many dead squirrels, but rarely do I see a dead turtle. Why? Because the squirrel is more easily excited and darts here and there, while the turtle remains still and retreats into his shell. You know where the turtle stands. Therefore, you can more easily avoid running over him.

Why does the squirrel dart here and there? Perhaps the sound of vibration or the oncoming auto excites him and prompts him to run to and fro. He lets his emotions get the best of him. The turtle remains in one place and stays in control, even though he might be just as frightened as the squirrel. He takes advantage of his protection—his shell.

Are you a squirrel or a turtle? Does the sound and

furor of the critics cause your head to spin and your body to fly out of control? Are you easily influenced by the people with whom you live? Do the voices of others motivate you to do those things which can bring happiness or even death to you? If so, you are like the squirrel. But you don't have to be!

You can be like the turtle. You know where you stand. The Lord Jesus Christ is your protection when the winds of the world begin to blow and the voices begin to tell you what you can and what you cannot do. You can say, "I know whom I have believed and am persuaded that he is able to keep that which I have committed unto him against that day" (II Timothy 1:12). You can say, "I can do all things through Christ who strengthens me" (Philippians 4:13). You can say, ". . . Greater is he that is in (me), than he that is in the world" (I John 4:40).

Our Weakness and His Strength Make an Unbeatable Combination

Darrel Anderson has written the following:

"The folklore surrounding Poland's famous concert pianist and prime minister, Ignace Paderewski, includes this story:

"A mother, wishing to encourage her young son's progress at the piano, bought tickets for a Paderewski performance. When the night arrived, they found their seats near the front of the concert hall and eyed the majestic Steinway waiting on stage.

"Soon the mother found a friend to talk to, and the boy slipped away. When eight o'clock arrived, the spotlights came on, the audience quieted, and only then did they notice the boy up on the bench innocently picking out 'Twinkle, Twinkle, Little Star.'

"His mother gasped, but before she could retrieve

her son, the master appeared on the stage and quickly moved to the keyboard.

"'Don't quit—keep playing,' he whispered to the boy. Leaning over, Paderewski reached down with his left hand and began filling in a bass part. Soon his right arm reached around the other side, encircling the child, to add a running obligato. Together, the old master and the young novice held the crowd mesmerized.

"In our lives, unpolished though we may be, it is the Master who surrounds us and whispers in our ear, time and again, 'Don't quit—keep playing.' And as we do, he augments and supplements until a work of amazing beauty is created" (Darrel L. Anderson, *Teenage Christian*).

Your first goal might be a "Twinkle, Twinkle, Little Star" goal, but it doesn't matter. You are playing with the Master, and the more you pursue your goals and reach them, the more you become like Him. "But, we all, with open face beholding as in a glass the glory of the Lord, are changed into the same image from glory to glory, even as by the Spirit of the Lord" (II Corinthians 3:18).

Can you believe it? Every day and in every way, you are beginning to look more and more like Jesus. You are in the process of changing. When you became a Christian, you changed. Now you are changing even more, and the change is beautiful!

There is Power in a Goal

A mother went to the doctor because her daughter was sick. The receptionist said that the doctor was too busy to see her. She barged on in and pleaded with the doctor. He ignored her. She kept on pleading. He told her that she was not one of his patients. She kept on pleading, and he called her a dog. She kept on pleading. He healed her daughter.

This remarkable story is found in the Bible (Matthew 15, Mark 7). Jesus complimented this woman when He said, "Great is thy faith."

What caused this woman to keep on asking when the disciples of Christ discouraged her? What caused her to keep on pleading when Jesus did not immediately answer her request?

She had a goal that was greater than her feelings! A goal will keep you going when even good people criticize you. A burning desire will keep you going when you are rejected. A specific goal will keep you going when you meet opposition, as she did. She had a goal—the healing of her daughter. She desired the healing of her daughter more than she desired protection of her feelings.

A goal will give you the power to persist. It will cause you to stick to it, no matter what. It will give you power never to give up. Have you ever enjoyed the feeling of succeeding in something? There is no feeling like the joy of accomplishment. You can do it!

Your goal is written down. You are saying it aloud. You are doing it every day. You are successful! You are growing! You are partners with God! Congratulations!

POWER TO FINISH

1. What are some of the mistakes Abraham and David made during their lifetimes? How did they finish life?
2. What are some of the challenges both of them faced which involved their sons, Isaac and Absalom? How did the fathers meet these challenges?
3. Consider one challenge you overcame.
4. What have you learned from that experience?
5. Evaluate this statement: "Every adversity carries with it an equal or greater benefit when we look for it."

6. What is one activity which required much time and effort to accomplish? What does this teach you about your present-day challenges?

CHAPTER 7

POWER TO GROW

How does a plant grow? Plant the seed in the ground. Then water, fertilize, cultivate, and reap the harvest.

How does a goal grow? The seed thought is planted in the mind. We water, fertilize, cultivate, and reap the harvest. We know this is true, because this is the way a man is born again. The seed—the word of God—is planted in his heart. That thought is cultivated, fertilized, and watered. "I have planted, Apollos watered, but God gave the increase" (I Corinthians 3:6).

How does a goal grow? First, it is planted in the mind. It is firmly entrenched in the mind by writing it down. There is great power in writing it down.

Decide What You Want to Plant

What do you want to grow in your life? What is your goal? A life without purpose is like giving a ball to two football teams on a field with no goal lines or posts. Confusion will reign! It is like playing basketball with no goals, just backboards. What will they do?

Where are you going? You say you are going to heaven. True, but there are several stops along the way. Life needs goals. What is your specific desire? What kind of person do you want to be?

Our children live in our homes, and we tell them what to do. But one day they leave the nest, and they are on their own. Decisions have to be made. *"What am I going to do? What school will I attend? What studies will I pursue? What am I going to be?"* These are not easy decisions, but they must be made.

God is nudging you out of the nest. He is asking you to ask, seek, and knock. Believe that a work is waiting for you. Begin now to set goals and really live and grow.

> Your mind is a garden,
> Your thoughts are the seeds,
> Your harvest will be
> Either flowers or weeds.
> —Mel Weldon

Have you ever noticed how the weeds seem to grow in a field without any encouragement? I have observed weeds that grew as large as trees, even with very little rainfall. Other plants were wilting, but the weeds were prospering.

However, the good seed has to be planted and cared for before it will grow. Concentrated effort must be exerted to receive a good harvest. You can grow! You are where you are and what you are because of your thought habits. Your thought habits grow from the food your mind feeds upon. You are in control! God has given you great power—the power to grow.

Beginning is half done! If you have not yet begun, you can do it now. Here are some suggestions of seed thoughts you can write down and let begin to grow in the garden of your mind. These are practical, and designed for all ages.

I will read one page in the Bible today.

I will say a kind word to someone today.

I will pray to God at 6:30 today.

I will take out the garbage today.

I will make up my bed today.

I will be on time for work today.

I will smile at someone who doesn't smile at me first today.

I will do my homework today.

I will talk to a shut-in today.

I will brush my teeth twice today.

I will say something encouraging to my mate today.

I will compliment someone at work today.

I will work with a cheerful spirit today.

I will compliment my children today.

I will say "I love you" to someone today.

I will give a tract to someone this week.

I will pray for my critics today.

I will listen to the teacher today.

I will walk one mile today.

I will pay my debts on time.

I will share some good news with someone today.

I will write a letter to my grandparents today.

I will thank my parents today.

I will give thanks to the one who prepared the food today.

I will say an encouraging word to the waitress in the restaurant today.

I will give thanks to God for my food at every meal.

I will visit and talk with an elderly person once each week.

I will say an encouraging word to a teen once each week.

I will rejoice and be glad when I awaken each day.

I will count my blessings when I pillow my head each night.

I will listen to others before speaking today.

Decide what you want and go after it.

"I believe I can meet my goal without writing it

down." You can. But it will secure your resolve when you write it down. We might compare writing it down to packing clothes in a suitcase and locking them in. You can carry them in a suitcase without locking it, but you will be more likely to lose them. Writing a goal down is like hearing a name more than once and repeating it to yourself. You will be able to remember the name easily. Writing secures the goal in your mind.

Congratulations! You have written it down! Now you are ready to grow and prosper!

Water and Fertilize Your Seed Thought

How do you water and fertilize a goal which you have written down? *Say it aloud!* That's right. Say it aloud every day. Say it every morning when you get up and every night before you go to bed.

"You make it sound too simple. Just write it down. Then read it aloud. I can't see the power in doing such simple things."

It is true. It is a simple thing to do. Is there really power in what you say? There is power in prayer! Prayer is what you say to God. Therefore, there is power in what you say.

Jesus said, ". . . your Father knows what things you have need of, before you ask him" (Matthew 6:8). If God knows our needs before we ask Him, then why ask Him? Why not just think them? Why not just meditate on them? Because Jesus said, "When you pray, say . . ." (Luke 11:2).

I have searched the Scripture for an example of prayer without words being formed. I have looked for an example of silent prayer and have found none. Eli did not hear Hannah praying, but she was forming the words (I Samuel 1:13). There is power in verbalizing your feelings to God. This point does not discount the power of meditation. It exalts the power of saying the prayer aloud.

A neurosurgeon states that the speech center in the brain rules over all the nerves in the body. If this is true, it exalts the power of speech to aid the body in doing what it needs to do. We know that the world was created by speech. We know that the gospel of Christ is to be spoken to the people of the world. Speech is a powerful medium.

I attended a business seminar in which the guest speaker asked for two volunteers—a strong, athletic young man and a small young lady. They came to the stage. He asked the young man to hold out his right arm with the palm down. He asked the young lady to stand behind the man near his right arm. He asked the young lady to take her right hand and push down on the man's arm as hard as she could when he repeated the statement for the third time. The statement was "I'm a loser, I'm a loser, I'm a loser." On the third statement, she pushed his arm and down it went.

Instructions were given to the man again. This time he was asked to repeat these words, "I'm a winner, I'm a winner, I'm a winner." The man did this, she pushed down on his arm, and the arm stood like granite. What made the difference? There is power in what you say!

"Wait a minute. That must have been a trick!" It was no trick. I have done this experiment several times, and those whom I have instructed have succeeded in doing it the first time they attempted it.

People have actually been known to begin feeling weak and sickly because others have suggested that they were looking sickly. The emotions and nerves in the human body are influenced by words. Words can cause anger and emotional unheaval. Words also have the power to calm and comfort.

You still want proof? Here it is! Jesus had spoken to and cursed the fig tree. The next day it was dried up from the roots. Peter marvelled. Jesus said, "Have faith in God. For verily I say unto you, that whosoever shall say unto this mountain, 'Be thou removed, and be thou cast into the sea,' and shall not doubt in his heart, but shall believe those things which he says shall come to pass: he shall have whatsoever he says" (Mark 11:22-23). Jesus said, "Say it, say it, say it, and it will happen for you!"

"Wait a minute! He was talking about speaking to a mountain and getting it to move. That's a miracle!"

It is true that the apostles could perform incredible miracles. But notice what Christ said in the record of Luke. "If you had faith as a grain of mustard seed, you might say unto this sycamine tree, 'Be thou plucked up by the root, and be thou planted in the sea;' and it should obey you" (Luke 17:6). That sounds like a miracle, doesn't it? But Jesus was applying it to a non-miraculous act—the act of forgiving your brother when he has sinned against you seven times in one day (Luke 17:4). Upon hearing this, the apostles said, "Lord, increase our faith." Then He gave the illustration of speaking to the sycamine tree.

My point is this. You can hire a bulldozer to move a mountain and a gardener to move a tree, but you can't get anyone to forgive someone for you. You have to find that in your own heart. Jesus used a miraculous illustration to motivate us to believe we can act in a non-miraculous situation. For this reason, I believe what Jesus said is a good illustration for us today. There is power in saying what you want and in believing that it can happen for you.

There is power in saying the words. You can plant seed thoughts in your own garden. You can make things grow by saying them and securing them in your mind. What a fantastic power! This does not mean that you get everything you say, but it does aid the doing and receiving of it.

Jesus said, "Ask, and it shall be given you; seek, and you shall find; knock, and it shall be opened unto you: For everyone that asks receives; and he that seeks finds; and to him that knocks it shall be opened" (Matthew 7:7,8). James said: "You have not, because you ask not."

What do you want? What do you see yourself becoming? What kind of a person do you want to be? Ask and you shall receive. This is the promise of God.

Say It in the Present Tense

How do you make a seed thought grow in your heart? Write it down. Say it aloud. Say it as if the thought has already occurred.

"Where do you get the idea to say it as if it has already happened?" The Bible, that's where! As Jesus talked about the mountain-moving faith and the power of saying it, he continued: "Therefore I say unto you, all things whatsoever you pray and ask for, believe that you have received them, and you shall have them" (Mark 11:24 American Standard Version).

We must see it in our minds before we have it in our hands. We must visualize it before it will come to reality. He is not saying that we actually have it, but he is saying to believe that we have it, and it will be ours.

This concept has been demonstrated in my life and in the lives of many others time and time again.

Recently I saw a film entitled *The Miracle Man.* He was called the Miracle Man because of his remarkable recovery from a terrible plane crash. His back was broken and crushed beyond repair. The doctors said that he would be a vegetable the remainder of his life.

Mr. Morris Goodman heard the specialists discussing his future and decided that he would do something to prove their predictions wrong. He was on a breathing machine. They said he would never breathe on his own again. He was fed intravenously. They said he would never be able to feed himself.

He had lost his ability to talk. They said he would never talk again. He was flat on his back. They said he would never walk again.

Mr. Morris had been taught the power of visualization in his profession. He began immediately to visualize himself breathing without the aid of a machine. He practiced breathing for days, as if he were not on the machine.

He and the nurse developed a code of speaking through the blinking of his eyes. He was taken off the machine for a few seconds. He breathed without any help. They marvelled at his ability to do so.

His next step was to feed himself. He visualized in his mind the chewing and digestion of food. He asked the nurse to get him a drink. She complied, and he drank it. The doctors scolded, "You could have strangled." "But I didn't," he blinked.

His next goal was to talk again. Talking was very painful, but he imagined himself conversing with his nurse. It was very painful as he made sounds like a baby at first. But then words began to form. He could talk! The doctors were amazed because damage had been done to his vocal cords.

His final goal was to walk out of the hospital. He saw himself walking into the doctor's office for a checkup the next month after release. He worked out in therapy every day. Still he could not walk.

The day came for his release. They were wheeling him to the front entrance when he stopped the wheelchair. He pushed himself up, took a step forward, and fell back into the chair. He pushed himself up again, took one step, then two, three, and fell against the front door of the hospital.

When he came for his monthly checkup, he walked

into the doctor's office. He was, indeed, the "miracle man!"

Was it a miracle or was it the power of the human mind to visualize and program the body for achievement and growth? I believe it was the latter.

Jesus said, "Believe it, say it, pray it, see it, and it is yours!" What do you want? What are you praying about? What are you doing to bring it to reality? Can you see it in your mind's eye? .

"I can't see acting as if I already have something before I receive it." I believe you can! Many of us operate on this principle each week. For example, I bought something with my credit card this month which I will pay for next month. I am acting by faith that my income will be adequate to make that payment at the proper time.

"But I know I am going to be paid at the end of the week. Therefore, I have no fear about paying for it." How do you know you are going to be paid? How do you know you will have a job at the end of the week? How do you know your company will continue beyond this month? We believe because of our experiences. Our faith is built to purchase something on credit because of past experiences.

This same type of faith can be centered in Jesus, who will help you to accomplish that which you have visualized and believed in your mind. You can draw on His power bank just as you draw on your salary in advance through the use of credit. The real question is what do you want? Decide what you want, write it down, say it aloud, and say it in the present tense— enthusiastically!

For example, instead of saying, "I will say a kind word to someone today," say, "I enjoy saying a kind word to someone every day." Instead of saying, "I will pray for my boss every day," say, "I am praying for my boss every day." You get the idea!

You Can Say It in Spite of Criticism

Doug Hooper coached a little league team that was not playing well in the play-offs. He tried a little act-as-if philosophy. He called them into the huddle and said, "Boys, I want you to pretend you have already hit three home runs off this pitcher, and you are coming to bat for the fourth time. What confidence you have! See yourself going up to that plate and hitting your fourth home run!" They all shouted "Yeaaaaa, let's do it!" Then a little voice piped up in the back, "Suppose they change pitchers!"

It does make a difference, you know. The new pitcher will be rested. He may be able to throw the ball faster. He will be different from the first. It is logical.

This is what people will do to you when you announce your goal. They will throw logic at you. "You can't do that." "You've never done that before." "Who do you think you are?" "You're too old to learn!"

This is the reason why you do not announce your goal to anyone except those who will encourage you in it. Share it only with those who will say, "Go to it! You can do it!"

The world preaches doubt; Jesus preaches faith. The world preaches fear; Christ preaches confidence. "Fear knocked at the door; faith answered, and no one was there." "This is the victory that overcomes the world, even our faith" (I John 5:4).

When you go to Memphis, Tennessee, visit the Pink Palace museum, former home of Clarence Saunders. In one corner of that museum is a small store, the first supermarket.

Clarence worked for a merchant in Memphis, and he was a dreamer. His boss told him, "Clarence, if you propose one more *hare*-brain idea to me, you're fired!"

Clarence went to lunch one day and saw a line of people in front of a new restaurant. He waited in line and went through his first self-service cafeteria. He rushed back to his boss and said, "Boss, you've got to see this . . . ." His boss stopped him in his tracks with these words, "Clarence, you're fired!" "You can't fire me—I resign!" said Clarence.

Clarence shared his idea with a company called Piggly Wiggly. They became the first supermarket chain.

Clarence's boss later told a reporter, "You know, every word I spoke in firing Clarence Saunders cost me a million dollars."

Dream a dream! Share that dream with others who dream. Do something about it! Set a goal. Get started on it. Don't quit! Say it aloud. Say it in the present tense with enthusiasm! You can do it!

"Now unto him that is able to do exceeding abundantly above all that we ask or think, according to the power that worketh in us, unto him be glory in the church by Christ Jesus throughout all ages, world without end. Amen" (Ephesians 3:21).

POWER TO GROW

1. What is one goal you have accomplished in your life? Relate the seed thoughts that caused it to happen.
2. What are deeds you can do today that would carry the impact of a miracle which Jesus performed (John 14:12)?
3. Relate three incidents in the life of Christ which were powerful in their influence when no miracle was performed.
4. Give a personal experience of the power of prayer in your life.
5. What influence do prayers of others have in your life?

CHAPTER 8

POWER TO IMITATE

How did the first disciples of Jesus grow? What power did they possess? It is true that they had the power to perform miracles, but this did not give them moral power. Judas was an example of moral power failure.

"And he ordained twelve, that they should be with him, and that he might send them forth to preach, and to have power to heal sicknesses, and to cast out devils . . ." (Mark 3:14).

In my presentations I ask this question: "Why did Jesus ordain twelve?" Three-fourths of the time, the answer is "to preach, heal sicknesses, and cast out devils." Many times the phrase "that they might be with him" is passed over. Yet, it is the first reason given.

When Jesus had gone back to heaven and the apostles were preaching the good news of salvation through Him, they received a compliment from their enemies. "Now when they saw the boldness of Peter and John, and perceived that they were unlearned and ignorant men, they marvelled; and they took knowledge of them that they had been with Jesus" (Acts 4:12).

In the Old Testament we read of men who walked with God. Yet, the apostles were the first men permitted to walk with God clothed in human flesh (John 1:1,14). Jesus said, ". . . he that has seen me has seen the Father . . ." (John 14:9).

It has been said that 93 percent of what we learn is through body posture. If this is true, then it is extremely important that we associate with those who exemplify the spirit of Christ.

The Disciples Learn a Hard Lesson

John the Baptist, Jesus, and His disciples taught that "the kingdom of heaven is at hand." To the average disciple of Christ, the kingdom of heaven meant that the Jews would reign as they did in the days of Saul, David and Solomon. In other words, the Jewish nation would be respected by the world once again. And they would no longer be under the rule of Rome.

Jesus spoke frequently of the growth of the kingdom, the value of the kingdom, and the power of the kingdom (Matthew 16:19; 13:31,32,44-46). He spoke of the exaltation of the twelve in the kingdom when they would "sit upon twelve thrones, judging the twelve tribes of Israel" (Matthew 19:28).

Because of their history and these words of Jesus, they visualized themselves as being clothed with power in the up-and-coming kingdom of Christ. They discussed their positions in the kingdom (Mark 9:34, Matthew 20:20). They were still discussing this in the upper room just a few hours before His betrayal (Luke 22:24).

How could He get them to see what He had been telling them? He had taken a child and pointed out that one must assume the humility of a little child in order to be great (Matthew 18:1-3). Then He taught that they were not to be like the great men of their day and time, but servants to all as He came to be

(Matthew 20:25-28). Still they argued about the positions of power. What could He do? What body posture could He assume?

He took a towel. He took water. He washed the feet of the apostles. He dried them with His towel. They were shocked. They were speechless—all except Peter.

The lesson was taught. They never forgot it. The king had come down from the throne. He had acted as a slave. They became servants. "If I then, your Lord and Master, have washed your feet, you also ought to wash one another's feet. For I have given you an example, that you should do as I have done to you" (John 13:14,15).

An example! That's what people are looking for! We do what we watch others do.

A daughter asked her mother, "Why do you cut the end off your ham before you put it in the oven?" The mother replied, "I don't know. That's the way my mother always did it." She called her mother on the phone that same day. "Mother, why did you always cut the end of your ham before you put it in the oven?" The reply was, "Because my pan wasn't long enough." We tend to duplicate what others do, regardless of the reasons.

A first-grade teacher walked from her classroom to the assembly with all of her children in a line directly behind her. She walked with a stiff left leg. Thirty-two little ones walked behind her, every one of them with a stiff left leg!

We Have the Power to Imitate

Rich Little has made a fortune imitating celebrities. We can imitate also, perhaps to a lesser degree. We even do it unconsciously, unaware of the influence of those with whom we associate.

What we would like to do is to imitate the best in

people through a conscious effort on our part. We do not want to be clones, but we do need a model or a mentor to follow.

"I don't want to imitate anyone! I want to do my own thing!" This is well and good, but you *will* imitate someone. You will follow someone's leading. The question is, who will it be? You have a choice in the matter.

The apostle Paul addressed this subject on several occasions. ". . .Be ye followers of me. . . . Be ye followers of me, even as I also am of Christ . . ." (I Corinthians 4:16; 11:1). Other translations say "imitators of me" or "Follow my example as I follow the example of Christ." "Brethren, be followers together of me . . . as you have us for an example" (Philippians 3:17). One translation says, "We have set the right example for you." "Those things, which you have both learned, and received, and heard, and seen in me, do (put into practice) and the God of peace shall be with you" (Philippians 4:9). "And you became followers of us, and of the Lord, having received the word in much affliction, with joy of the Holy Ghost: so that you were examples to all that believe in Macedonia and Achaia" (I Thessalonians 1:6,7).

This is the way Christianity works. You follow an example, and you set an example for others to follow. "For you yourselves know how you ought to follow our example. We were not idle when we were with you, nor did we eat anyone's food without paying for it. On the contrary, we worked night and day, laboring and toiling so that we would not be a burden to any of you. We did this, not because we do not have the right to such help, but in order to make ourselves a model for you to follow" (II Thessalonians 3:7-9).

Paul was an example, and he challenged Timothy and Titus to be examples to others. "Let no man despise your youth; but be an example of the believers, in word, in behavior, in love, in spirit, in faith, in purity." "Encourage the young men to be self-controlled: in everything set them an example by doing what is good" (I Timothy 4:12; Titus 2:6,7).

Paul, an unmarried man, was not telling God's people to follow him in celibacy. Paul, the preacher, was not instructing everyone to become preachers and missionaries. Paul, the tentmaker, was not binding that occupation on everyone else.

He was encouraging them to adopt his spirit of humility, brotherly love, dependence on Christ, and industry.

Think about the people who have influenced your lives for good—parents, teachers, classmates, marriage partners, children, business associates, kinspeople, grandparents, preachers, brethren, recreational partners, employees, employers, and fellow workers. You are a composite of all with whom you have come in contact, for better or worse.

You can be greater than you are! Greatness and success depends on whom you choose to associate with in the future. You want to be a winner? Associate with winners. You want to be a teacher? Select a good teacher as a model. You want to be a doctor? Get a job at the hospital and work closely with the doctors whom you consider to be outstanding. Observe them and listen to them. You want to be a cook? Begin working with a cook whom you admire. You want to become successful in business? Select a successful businessman to work for and go after that job, especially in the field of your choice.

Steve Orgain wants to be a great song director. For years he has followed and listened to Ray Walker, one of the greatest. He watches Ray direct singing in person. He listens to him for hours at a time on tape. He says that he can turn the tape on in his mind and hear Ray sing. This power to imitate has helped Steve to become an outstanding song director.

We were having song drill at church one night, and

someone asked Steve to lead a song he had never led before. His response was, "I heard Grandpa Jones, the entertainer, sing this song once before. I'm not sure I can." I encouraged him to try it. He did it well.

After church was dismissed, I complimented him. He replied, "I could see Grandpa Jones standing by my side, singing that song. I just sang along with him." This is a tribute to the power of imitation and visualization. Find the best people and begin to duplicate the best qualities in them.

While visiting in Mobile, Alabama, I heard Marshall Underwood deliver a masterpiece on the subject of prayer. In that sermon he told how his mother always prayed at his bedside every night for thirteen years until her death. I never heard Marshall pray, but I know from the message he delivered that he was a praying man. His mother had taught him by example.

Timothy's father was not a Christian. But his mother and grandmother were. From them the sincere faith was ignited in this young man, God's preacher (II Timothy 1:5).

Jim Higdon remembers when he could not offer a public prayer in church. He began to overcome this problem by going with an experienced teacher into the homes of others. Jim would talk about the weather, sports, or the news. His friend would teach them about Christ. Soon Jim began to share the message of Christ also. He learned to share through watching and listening to another. Today, Jim can preach, and he is enrolled in a school for ministers one night each week.

What Role Models Have Done for Me

From my earliest memories I was taught to read. I knew how to read before I entered the first grade. My mother was the teacher.

My mother has always believed in me. When I was in

the sixth-grade program, I forgot a prayer which I had memorized. This was devastating! When I was in the ninth grade I forgot a speech which I was supposed to deliver. But my mother still believed in me.

When I was in high school, my speech teacher, Vivian Pierce, believed in me. My principal, Mitchell Bennett, was a great master of ceremonies. He could make the announcements sound exciting. He encouraged me in sports and cheered me on. When I began at David Lipscomb College, many of the teachers expressed their belief in me and encouraged me to preach.

My wife, Ruth, believes in me. She has always believed in me. She has been a great example for me in hard work and a desire to get something done now.

When I began preaching, I had received training from and had heard the best. I continued to read and listen to the best. I associate with preachers and brethren who exemplify the spirit of Christ. Why? Because we are the body of Christ, and I want to look as much like Jesus as possible.

Jesus said, "You are the light of the world." When He said that, He was looking through the centuries at you and me.

How do you become light? The Bible says, "You are light in the Lord . . ." (Ephesians 5:8). One of the ways that we become light is by associating with light. "For light is capable of showing up everything for what it really is. It is even possible for light to turn the thing it shines upon into light also" (Ephesians 5:13, Phillips). "Let your light so shine before men, that they may see your good works, and glorify your Father which is in heaven" (Matthew 5:16).

I have known Billy Clark since he was a young man in Giles County, Tennessee. At that time, he had an operation on his brain and was an invalid. Our paths did not cross until ten years later when we moved to

Dickson, Tennessee, where he and his mother were living. He was legally blind and could read Braille. He spent much of his time flat on his back or in a wheelchair. He had experienced seven brain surgeries.

Then his mother died, and he was left alone. His uncle had him placed in a local nursing home, where we visited with him each week. He always had a cheery disposition. An outstanding doctor said he would be a vegetable the remainder of his life.

Billy made the decision to move to Nashville into an apartment of his own. His uncle wanted him to stay where he was secure and had the best of care. But Billy was persistent.

Today Billy is self-sufficient in a teacher's retirement apartment home. He can feed and bathe himself. He can use the telephone with ease. He can enjoy a party and make you feel good when you visit with him. He believes there is a job waiting for him somewhere out there in the world. He believes in God, and he believes in himself.

His example of light has caused me to burn more brightly. He is my model in persistence.

You Can Choose a Model to Imitate

When Nashville businessman Don Northcutt was a student in college, he was on probation because of his grades. One day after class, a stewardess requested, "Don, will you study with me for the final test? You seem to know what the professor is talking about." His comments in class had impressed her.

Don thought to himself, "If she believes in me, why can't I believe in me?"

It was customary for the professor to read the final test grades beginning with the highest marks. He began, "It is an honor to read this first name—Don

Northcutt." "The next month I made the Dean's List," beamed Don, as he told this story to me.

Don added, "That was the turning point in my life. What that attractive young lady said to me changed my self image."

When you choose examples and let them know that they are an inspiration to you, you can bless their lives also.

Job must have been a great example. His friend testified, "Your words have kept men on their feet" (Job 4:4, Moffitt's Trans.).

Look for men and women whose words will keep you on your toes. Look for a mate in life who will help you develop the spirit of Christ. Look for a boss who is an example of industry and vision and integrity. Look for a friend who will build you up and not tear you down.

You are Changing Day by Day

Transformation occurs through the process of beholding. Moses beheld the glory of the Lord, and his face radiated that encounter. The Bible says, ". . . We all . . . beholding . . . the glory of the Lord, are changed into the same image from glory to glory, even as by the Spirit of the Lord" (II Corinthians 3:18).

We see Jesus in the Bible. We see the Lord in the lives of His people, the church, the body of Christ. Every day you are changing as you associate with the Christ of the Bible and His body on earth—the church.

"I can see the change in others, but I haven't noticed any in me." One of the amusing things about attending a class reunion is to observe how much older others look when I haven't changed at all. You see, I am with me all the time, and I don't notice the changes that take place. Take it from me. You are changing as you walk with the Lord in the Bible and with your role models in the church. The Bible says the change is gradual, "from one degree of glory to another." Believe it and rejoice!

POWER TO IMITATE

1. What characteristics of your parents do you see in yourself?
2. What qualities in your church leaders do you admire most?
3. Telephone or write the one teacher in school who had the greatest influence on you. Express your appreciation to him.
4. Express your gratitude to someone in your family for the outstanding example he has been for you in one specific area of your life.
5. What is the distinction between copying and imitating some person you admire?
6. Investigate the differences between real life experiences and the way life is depicted on TV in fictional programs. Examples: "I need a drink!" in stressful situations; frequency of pre-marital and extra-marital sex; absence of spiritual atmosphere in the homes—prayers, Bible readings, gratitude expressed to God, honor to Christ.

CHAPTER 9

POWER TO GIVE

"He who sows sparingly shall reap also sparingly; and he who sows bountifully shall reap also bountifully" (II Corinthians 9:6).

The headlines read, "Retiring Jeweler Remembers Elvis." Mr. Harry Levitch was the personal jeweler of Elvis Presley. How did he get to know his most famous customer? He told it this way:

"My wife and I have over the years operated a sort of unofficial student aid fund. One day the principal of Humes called me and told me he had a kid that had torn clothes and run-down shoes and no place to get more. So I got the kid some clothes. He lived in Hurt Village.

Not long after, this tall, good-looking young man walked in, shook my hand, and said, 'Mr. Levitch, you don't know me. My name is Elvis Presley, and someday I'm gonna be famous. And when I am, you'll be my jeweler, because you helped my friend, Red West.' (*The Commercial Appeal*, Memphis, Saturday, February 8, 1986).

Elvis Presley was a very generous person. If he liked someone, he would give them either a Cadillac or a diamond ring. How would you like to have been his jeweler?

You reap what you sow. Mr. Levitch sowed benevolence and reaped business and profit.

A trucker friend of mine helped a fellow trucker in time of financial need. This friend in need lived in Mississippi and became quite prosperous. Years later, my friend was facing bankruptcy. The friend he had helped years ago called, offered him a job, and rescued my friend from financial ruin. You reap what you sow.

Charles Harvey, from Grand Prairie, Texas, felt a bit nervous as he was driving to an important job interview. He was fifteen minutes late when he passed a middle-aged woman stranded with a flat tire. "My conscience made me stop. I changed her tire and headed for the interview, thinking I could just forget about the job."

But he filled out the job application anyway and went to the personnel director's office. Did he get the job? He sure did. The personnel director hired him on the spot. She was the woman whose tire he had just changed! You reap what you sow!

You Reap More than You Sow

In my hand I am holding an ear of corn. How many grains of corn were planted to produce this one ear? Only one! I have counted the number of grains on this one ear. Seven hundred grains! In all probability there was another ear on the same stalk. Fourteen hundred grains from one seed—that's a good investment. So when you plant, don't be stingy with the seed!

When I was nineteen, during the summer months I worked for Southwestern Publishing Company while attending college. We sold Bibles and other books door to door.

After the first week, I saw that the Lord was

prospering me in a wonderful way. Even though we
were on our own, had no salary, and lived on our down
payments, I made the decision to give twenty dollars to
the church every Sunday. Twenty dollars then was like
eighty dollars now. At the end of the summer I had
prospered so much, the last two Sundays I gave eighty
dollars per week. You reap more than you sow!

Put God to the Test

The Bible says, ". . . Prove me now . . . says the Lord
of hosts, if I will not open the windows of heaven, and
pour you out a blessing, that there shall not be room
enough to receive it" (Malachi 3:10). The first part of
this verse challenges you to give and put God to the
test.

How do you make room to receive the gifts of God?
How would you make room to receive new furniture for
your home? You could give the old furniture away.
That's the way you make room for God's blessings.
Give away what you have now!

In challenging us to be cheerful givers, the Bible
says: "And God is able to make all grace abound toward
you; that you, always, having all sufficiency in all
things, may abound to every (or all) good work"
(II Corinthians 9:8).

Five times in this verse the word *"all"* or its
equivalent is found. Do you get the idea that God is
ready to shovel it in when you shovel it out?

In my mind is the image of a corn scoop dipping
into a storage crib. The more I shovel out, the more
the windows of heaven are open to fill it again to
overflowing. Do you want the blessings of God? Begin
now to share with others.

Mr. and Mrs. M. C. Pippin of Vanleer, Tennessee, put
God to the test. When Mr. Pippin was disabled for six

months and unable to draw disability because of the nature of the accident, he and his wife made a decision. They decided to continue giving to the Lord the identical amount they had been giving, even though he was drawing no salary during that period of time.

Mr. Pippin declares, "We were prospered more during that six-month period than if we had been drawing a salary. Some people who owed money to us paid their debts during that period of time, even though they did not know our circumstances."

Give and It Shall Be Given unto You

God has promised, "Give and it shall be given unto you; good measure, pressed down, and shaken together, and running over, shall men give into your bosom" (Luke 6:38).

Everyone likes to receive good measure when he's buying or trading. This is the principle on which the Lord works. You give and you always receive more than you give.

"I know I am going to have treasures in heaven; that's more than I'll ever receive here on earth."

But that isn't what this verse is talking about. Jesus is talking about the here and now!

Read again the latter part of the verse, ". . . shall men give into your bosom." Men give here and now!

When Peter asked Jesus about the reward for following Him, the gracious response was, "Verily I say unto you, there is no man that has left house, or brethren, or sisters, or father, or mother, or wife, or children, or lands, for my sake, and the gospel's, but he shall receive an hundredfold now in this time, houses, and brethren, and sisters, and mothers, and children, and lands, with persecutions; and in the world to come eternal life" (Mark 10:29,30).

Jesus said there are two rewards—one in this life and one in the world to come. Believe this promise and share your life with others!

In the context of the promise of Jesus, "Give, and it shall be given unto you," there are several challenges Jesus suggests to us. He suggests that we give the following:

love to our enemies,

prayer for those who oppose us,

good will to those who mistreat us,

goods to those who need them,

mercy to those who have offended,

kindness to the unthankful and evil (Luke 6:27-37). Some of these are more challenging to give than money, are they not?

You want to receive kindness. Give it. You want to receive a smile. Try smiling. You want forgiveness. Forgive. You want sympathy. Sympathize. You want friends. Be one. You want to make more money. Give more service. Go the second mile at your work.

It is important to understand that you reap what you sow. This does not mean that when you sow money, you always reap money. You might reap recognition, love, friendship and appreciation. On the other hand, some will sow deeds of kindness and reap money. Some might not need money or be able to handle it. The Lord will reward us in the way which is best for us.

You Can Know How Much You Will Receive

"Am I reading you correctly? Did you say you can know how much you will receive? How can this be?" You can be sure that you always receive more than you give! God does not want to be like us. Therefore, He always gives more. He wants us to be like Him. Therefore, He sets the example in giving.

Even though He does not duplicate our giving, we do have a voice in our own prosperity. Jesus says, "For with the same measure that you measure with, it shall be measured to you again" (Luke 6:38).

"Well, I'm doing all that I possibly can at the present time." You will feel differently about this when you begin to use a larger measure with which to give. Visualize yourself giving a bag of groceries to a needy family. You can be assured that the Lord will use a bag of similar size to bless you, with one difference—"good measure, pressed down, and shaken together, and running over . . . ." This is the promise of our Lord. You can't outgive Him. He has been in the business of giving longer than we ever will be.

God's greatest gift is found in these words: "For you know the grace of our Lord Jesus Christ, that, though he was rich, yet for your sakes he became poor, that you through his poverty might be rich" (II Corinthians 8:9). This motivation was given to encourage churches to help brethren who were in physical need. It is an encouragement for us to give through the church today. This is not the only way, but it is one of the ways approved by God.

"Upon the first day of the week let every one of you lay by him in store, as God has prospered him . . ." (I Corinthians 16:2). What a joy it is to share with brethren on the first day of every week! What a thrill it is to see parents teaching their youth to give out of what the Lord has given them the past week! In our giving we really imitate the Lord Jesus Christ.

"I would give more to the church, but I don't like the way the money is spent."

Jesus tells a story about a man with two sons (Luke 15). Some call this the story of the prodigal son. This prodigal son asked for his part of the inheritance, left home, and squandered it. Depression struck, and he found himself working in a pig pen without a bite to eat. He came to himself and went back home. The father was so happy, he threw a party for the son. When his brother came in from the field, he found out what was going on. He was angry and would not go in. Therefore, the father came out and encouraged him. The son's complaint was, "I don't like the way the money is being spent."

The father, who represents God, the Father, reminded him that he was dwelling on the negative. "Look at the good that is being done. Your brother was lost; now he is found. He was dead; now he is alive. All that I have is yours. You will not receive less because of the decision I am making with the money."

There are only two ways to do things—my way and their way. Some might not like my way if I were in charge of spending the Lord's money. The question we must ask is simple: "Is good being done with the gifts to the Lord?" If so, let us avoid a wrong attitude about the way money is spent. Remember, God will not prosper you less because of the way the money is invested. You will be blessed because you gave with the proper motive. Others will be judged by what they do with the money after it is placed in their hands. Isn't it wonderful how many good works can be done because brethren give generously and cooperate in the work of the church?

Consider the church in Corinth in the first century. They had many problems:
spirit of division,
law suits among themselves,
fornication,
unspiritual worship,
jealousy over gifts of God,
lack of consideration for each other,
false teaching about the resurrection.
Even so, the Lord called upon them to give upon the

first day of every week as they had been prospered. *"What? Give to a church that has all kinds of problems?"* That's what the Lord said. All of us have problems. Let us deal with them and continue to support good works at the same time.

How Much Should I Give?

There is a story which helps me with this challenge.

"And Jesus sat over against the treasury, and behold how the people cast money into the treasury: and many that were rich cast in much. And there came a certain poor widow, and she threw in two mites. . . .

"And he called his disciples, and said to them, Verily I say unto you, that this poor widow has cast more in than all they which have cast into the treasury:

"For all they did cast in of their abundance; but she of her want did cast in all that she had, even all her living" (Mark 12:41-44).

Two mites isn't much, is it? Yet the Lord said it was more than all of the other gifts put together. Why? Because he looks at what we give in comparison with what we have. You may think that your gift doesn't count much because it is not as large as the gifts of others. Jesus says, "And whosoever shall give to drink unto one of these little ones a cup of cold water only in the name of a disciple, verily I say unto you, he shall in no wise lose his reward" (Matthew 10:42). No gift is so small that it goes unnoticed by the Lord.

It is estimated that if the widow's mite had been deposited at the "First National Bank, Jerusalem" to draw four percent interest semi-annually, the fund today would total $4,800,000,000,000,000,000,000.

If a bank on earth could multiply the widow's mite to such an astronomical figure, think what treasures this dedicated woman will have in heaven where "moth and rust does not corrupt."

You Can Grow in Your Giving

I challenge you to grow in your giving as you grow in other areas of your walk with the Lord. "But just as you excel in everything—in faith, in speech, in knowledge, in complete earnestness, and in your love for us—see that you also excel in this grace of giving" (II Corinthians 8:7).

Are you growing in your giving of your money to the Lord? The verse just quoted specifies growth in this area. *"Well, I am giving more than I did five years ago."* That's good, but the question is: "Are you growing in your giving?"

Inflation has given many the power to give more, but it also has given the power to make more. One could give twice as much as ten years ago and still not be growing in giving. Why? Because your income might be twice as much! If so, you would be giving the same in proportion to what you are making. I challenge you to give a greater percentage to the Lord than you have been giving. I challenge you to give some more to the Lord, beginning now. "Remember this: whoever sows sparingly will also reap sparingly, and whoever sows generously will also reap generously" (II Corinthians 9:6).

The Greatest Gift You Can Give

Eleven people were imprisoned on a large ice floe in the north. It seems that a huge frozen block had broken loose from the land and was beginning to melt.

It threatened to sweep them down the river to their death.

The man relating this story said,

"My brother, learning of the situation, put fifty dollars in his pocket and rushed to the rescue. Arriving on the scene, he found many on the banks of the river waiting for the catastrophe which seemed inevitable. Stepping up to the crowd, he offered the fifty dollars to anyone who would attempt to help the imperiled ones, but not a person stirred.

"Obtaining a stout line, my brother tied one end of it around his waist and offered to join with anyone who would rope himself to him in the effort to rescue those who were in such dire jeopardy. Immediately four men leaped to his side. They roped themselves to the same line, and then the five of them, picking their way over a dangerous gorge at the hazard of their lives, brought every man, woman, and child on the ice floe to safety. When my brother offered money, not a man stirred; but when they saw him give himself, it drew them to his side in an instant."

At one village in Africa the custom was to draw a circle on the ground for the church gifts. Each one would bring his money, clothing, jewelry, or produce to share with the poor and to meet the needs of that congregation.

One young man who was a new convert had nothing but the clothing he wore. Without hesitation, he stepped into the circle himself.

We read of people from Macedonia who were generous beyond their ability to give. Paul reveals their spirit to us in these words, ". . .First, they gave themselves to the Lord . . ." (II Corinthians 8:5).

Here is the chain reaction. Christ gave Himself for

us. We give ourselves to Him. We give ourselves to others. It will be given unto us. This is the promise of God!

POWER TO GIVE

1. Search for several examples where Jesus gave special gifts which were not miraculous. In what ways were these gifts worth more than money?
2. What benefits do systematic and regular acts of giving provide?
3. Share an example from your life where (a) someone's gift to you motivated you to give and (b) someone's gift to others motivated you to give.
4. Who is the most generous person you know, and what type of gift does he or she primarily give?
5. Give examples from the Bible where men and women were highlighted and honored because of their gifts. How can we emulate the Holy Spirit's example in recording these acts of generosity today? In what ways can we show honor to generous people today? What are some guidelines in the Bible?
6. What is the greatest gift you have to offer to your fellow man? Discuss the gifts in Romans 12. Are they miraculous or non-miraculous?

CHAPTER 10

POWER TO SHARE

In the Sermon on the Mount, Jesus challenges us to increase our outreach. "For if you love them which love you, what reward have you? Do not even the publicans the same? And if you salute your brethren only, what do you more than others? Do not even the publicans so?" (Matthew 6:46,47).

It is easy to be with my loved ones and friends, but what about reaching out to others whom I do not know and with whom I have not developed a relationship? *I am fearful I will make a mistake,* you say. True, but the greatest mistake of all is to fail to venture out.

We Have Something in Common with Others

How did Jesus make friends and begin conversations with new people? Perhaps the best incident of all is the encounter of Christ with the woman at the well (John 4).

Seemingly, they had nothing in common. She was of the opposite sex. She was a Samaritan. She had a different religion. And she was a sinner. Yet, they had something in common—they both needed water. So He asked her for a drink of water. This surprised her. She recognized that He was different because He was willing to talk to her, even though most of His people would not.

While working for Southwestern, we were taught to ask for a drink of water as we distributed Bibles from door to door. Asking for a drink was not difficult to do, because we were walking and it was the hot summertime. But usually this request would give us a chance to share our products.

What do we have in common with others? What are things that people talk about? The local news and weather are probably talked about more than anything else.

We Can Learn from the World of Business

In the business world, there is a formula which is used to help one get acquainted with others. It is called FORM, and each letter stands for something which people enjoy talking about.

F—Family
O—Occupation
R—Recreation
M—Money

Suppose you meet someone at the supermarket. You are standing in line or selecting some fruit. Your introduce yourself and ask the person's name. You might ask about his children or grandchildren.

A gentleman was walking down the aisle of a bus questioning, "Do you have any grandchildren?" All answered in the affirmative, until one gentleman said no. The questioner replied, "Well, I want to sit by you and tell you about mine." How many times people have offered to show pictures of their children and grandchildren to me!

You might ask where a person works or what kind of recreation he enjoys? Perhaps he has on a jogging suit. You have a hint already about the person's recreational activities.

Of course, the money approach is designed by the business world to find out about financial needs. This part of the approach might not be applicable for that reason, but it is easy to break the ice with people when you talk about the price of groceries, clothing, or taxes. The important thing is that you establish a relationship, even though it is not an intimate one.

You Can Ask Questions

One of the best ways to get to know people is to ask questions—questions they would enjoy answering. Most people are interested in their families, their jobs, their vacations, their hobbies, their autos, their homes, their communities. Jesus was a master at asking questions.

To the man at the pool of Bethesda, who had been sick thirty-eight years, He asked, "Will you be made whole?" (John 5). He was interested in the lame man's health, and He did something about it.

To the man who had been born blind and who had developed tremendously in his faith the same day he was healed, Jesus asked, "Do you believe in the Son of God?" (John 9).

A lawyer asked the question, "Master, what must I do to inherit eternal life?" Jesus responded with the question, "What is written in the law? How do you read?" (Luke 10). The man was well-versed in the law, so Jesus permitted him to answer his own question. When the lawyer did this, he would be debating with himself.

You will notice that Jesus did not ask the same question of everyone. He examined a person's needs and asked a question which would serve him best.

Some people had not had the same experiences with Him as others. Therefore, He began with a different type of question for the occasion. He is our model in asking questions. It pays to know as much as possible about your new friend.

Magnify Their Importance by Writing It Down

After a first-time meeting with a new person, add his or her name to your list. Make a list of others, and keep it in a place where you can read it frequently. Add information about each person, especially the ones who are new friends. Are they married? How many children do they have? What are their names? How old are the children? Where do they go to school? What are the needs of these new friends? What do they want out of life? Do they have sickness in the family? Do they have a family member in the nursing home? Did they just lose a mate? Do they have a child who has special problems? Is their marriage a healthy one? Do they have financial challenges? How do they feel about themselves? How do they like where they live? Are they satisfied with their spiritual growth? You do not ask all of these questions, but in getting to know them you will learn some information.

What I am saying is to show a genuine interest in people because of your love for them and for Christ. Do not be nosy, but in as natural a way as possible introduce yourself, ask questions, and listen—really listen. You will be building a bridge to a closer relationship in the future.

You Can Pray for Your New Friends

A certain brother whom I admire told me that I am on his prayer list. I appreciate this. It lets me know that he is interested enough in me to introduce me into his conversation with his heavenly Father. That makes me feel important.

I don't know of anything that is more important in meeting new people than including them in our prayer life, especially when they request it. As we get to know them better and crises arise in their lives, they will be drawn to the one who has listened most attentively to them in times past. Our ultimate dream is that they will become our brothers and sisters in the family of God.

Where do you meet your future brothers and sisters? Jesus went into the market place, the wide, open spaces, the places of sickness, the homes where He was invited, and the synagogues.

You and I can go into the marketplace, the hospitals, private homes, prisons, schools, vacation lands, or wherever people are found. But there is one place we must not overlook, a place of great importance where our influence can be felt in a most powerful way. J. Goodspeed was taught this valuable lesson by a young mother. Here is his account of the schooling he received.

Staying with the Baggage

"A few years ago, a lovely Christian mother gave me criticism I deserved. I had preached a strong sermon on personal evangelism, pointing out every Christian's obligation to reach out and win others to the Lord. In the conclusion of the sermon, I tried to obliterate every excuse that anyone might have given for failure to lead others to Christ. The sermon needed to be preached, of course, as it still does. Apparently, however, I had been guilty of some unfair emphasis.

"After the sermon I was invited home with a lovely Christian family. The husband was completing his resident work as a medical doctor and had little spare time, but still (I might add) spent some of this time in our personal work program. The wife beautifully cared for their three lovely children. All of them were very young, one still an infant in arms who required a lot of time.

"During the meal the wife asked if I remembered the scripture: 'For as his share is who goes down into the battle, so shall his share be who stays by the baggage' (I Samuel 30:24).

"I confessed my ignorance, and she gave the context of King David's insisting that the home guard be rewarded equally with those who had the more obviously essential role of fighting in the front line.

"And then, she shared a wonderful truth with me that I'm sure I already knew, but had forgotten. She mentioned that she felt taking care of her children—patiently teaching them the ways of God and His great values, looking for moments of readiness to retrack them gently when they get on the wrong track—was staying with the baggage. She went on to point out that she often felt guilty for not doing more 'church' work that she did, but that she felt her greatest ministry was being a dedicated Christian mother.

"My friend, all you need to say after listening to a needed reprimand like that is one word . . . Amen" *(Joe Goodspeed)*.

God has given parents great power to mold and make children in His image. We need help to lead our children and to reach out to others. Jesus said, "Ask, and it shall be given unto you, seek, and you shall find; knock, and it shall be opened unto you:

"For everyone that asks, receives, and he that seeks, finds, and to him that knocks, it shall be opened" (Matthew 7:7,8).

"Now unto him that is able to do exceeding abundantly above all that we ask or think, according to the power that works in us, unto him be glory in the church by Christ Jesus throughout all ages, world without end. Amen" (Ephesians 3:20,21).

POWER TO SHARE

1. Why do you listen to others?
2. When do you listen to others?
3. How much do you listen to others? Take inventory of one day in your life and see if you listen more than you talk.
4. What does the discussion of gifts in Romans 12 teach about sharing Christ with others? What are the challenges we face in becoming more evangelistic?
5. In your opinion, what is the most important thing you can do to share Christ with others at the present time?
6. Does the statement, "I have planted, Apollos watered; but God gave the increase," have anything to offer to our evangelistic thrust?
7. What are some of the blessings which Barnabas shared? (Acts of the Apostles) From the example of Barnabas, what growth patterns, if any, can be observed? Do you know of anyone who has shared at one stage in his life, and this has led to sharing even more of his life with others? Could this be one of the ways God develops us today?